Be the change

FRAN CHERNY

# BE THE CHANGE

THE ART OF BECOMING
OUR OWN INNOVATION PROJECT

METRÓPOLIS
LIBROS

Cherny, Francisco
Be the change : the art of becoming our own innovation project / Francisco Cherny. - 1a ed - Ciudad Autónoma de Buenos Aires : Metrópolis Libros, 2021.
196 p. ; 23 x 16 cm.

Traducción de: Amber Isabel Aguilar.
ISBN 978-987-8924-07-6

1. Desarrollo Personal. I. Aguilar, Amber Isabel, trad. II. Título.
CDD 158.1

---


First edition, August 2021
First edition in English, February 2022

**Design and layout**
Lara Melamet

**Translator**
Amber Isabel Aguilar

**Editing**
Martín Vittón

**Proofreading**
Nicholas Basily

Printed in Argentina



**METRÓPOLIS**
LIBROS

**Metrópolis Libros is a publishing house of PAM! Publicaciones**
info@pampublicaciones.com.ar | www.pampublicaciones.com.ar

*For my parents, Alicia and Hugo,
without whom none of this would
have happened.*

# contents

# prologue

A fresh breeze on a hot London afternoon: the memory of the first time I met Fran, around ten years ago, evoked now by his book "Be the Change." Throughout my life and career, my concept of what work is has evolved considerably. What I initially viewed as a way to "earn a living," create value, or change the world around me, became a way to express my own individuality and creativity – and, based on that, a path to connecting with others and with the world, and now with myself, in a process of human growth. The path to this progress of seeing the working world through the lens of human resources and organizational development afforded me the chance to work with some brilliant people and enabled me to work with some whom I consider very special. And that's what happened with Fran. After countless conversations with consultants who specialized in corporate culture and change management, and a plethora of presentations on methods, structures and outlines that answered questions I hadn't even asked, Fran and his team opened up the right dialogue: a conversation charged with curiosity and genuine interest in what was truly important to me and my team. Being able to shine a light on what we were looking for enabled us to embark on exploration and dialogue together.

Many years later, the quality of Fran's focus still resounds with me. He takes on new challenges with fresh eyes, an open mind, and pure curiosity, rather than offering recycled, one-size-fits-all formulas. He is part of a small subset of professionals who don't hesitate to offer their profound experience with the open-mindedness of a novice, in order to experience the transformative power of profound work with others and on oneself.

In an era where all life and work formulas are subject to questioning, and the imposition of rigid restrictions may be as inopportune as the virus itself – we write during what we hope is the peak of a pandemic – it will be exploration itself that will keep us sane and spiritually balanced, rather than marking out a specific territory for ourselves.

It is this very exploration that you will find in Fran's book. Based on his personal and professional experiences, and recognizing all the interconnections between them, he brings us a collection not of recipes but of invitations to appreciate each ingredient fully. Through his narration of personal, professional, spiritual and genealogical stories, meta-reflections, inspirational quotes and practical exercises, he inspires us to reconsider how to lead the lives we want.

His unpretentious suggestions, so fluid and open, are the perfect travel companion for the reader's own pilgrimage, where shared experiences facilitate our own discoveries. It is a constant reminder that who we are, and who we want to be, is the result of our own choices: without intention, there is no awareness, and without awareness, there is no choice.

I always bear in mind that, when exploring the narrative of a new client who needs help changing something, Fran deftly challenges us with one fundamental question: "What really has you 'hooked' and is important to you?". In this book, Fran regales us with many such "hooks," trusting that the answer to his question lies within every one of us. All we have to do is dive down and find it.

**Paulo Pisano**
Senior Vice President and Chief People Officer at Booking.com

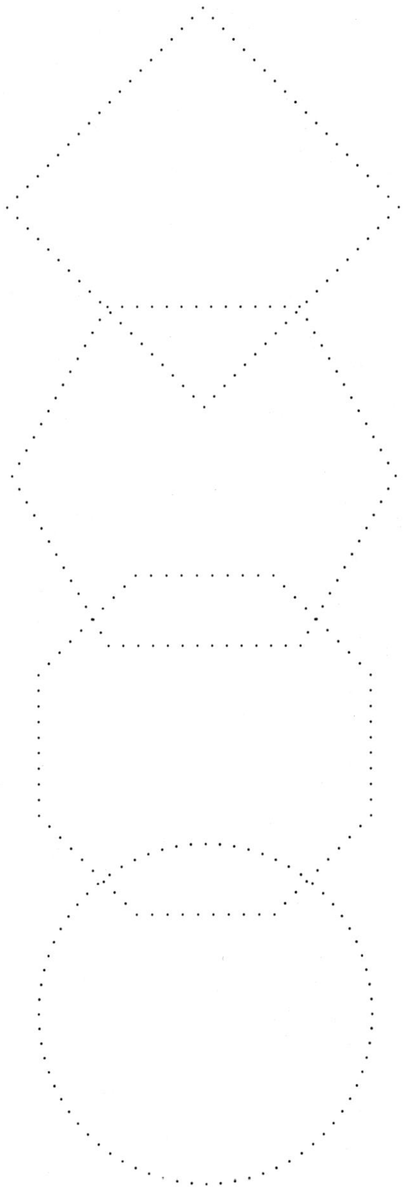

# introduction

# My invitation, your decision

I have had the enormous privilege of a life that showed me a variety of very different places, cultures and people. Thinkers and entrepreneurs, sceptics and believers, businesses, non-profit associations and neighborhood clubs. Ever since I could reason, multiculturality, diversity and the ability to explore new worlds have been present in my education.

Today, more than ever, I am grateful to my parents and to my parents' parents, right back to the beginning of my family tree, for the fact that this has been possible. The migration of my ancestors, their need to carve out new paths in foreign lands – and to do so while still acknowledging their history – may have prefaced my own experience in a world where people seek to find out which era of their history they are in.

This book aims to offer a look at the world we live in and how we can better interact with others during the years we spend here. It is the result of my own life experiences: exploring around thirty countries, living in four different cities, and working for over fifteen years alongside leaders of the widest-ranging global, regional and local companies.

This process started during my adolescence, when I entered work in the world of non-profit organizations, where joining people together was the driving factor. It continued when I went on to form part of the creative group of Axialent, which, over the course of its almost twenty years, has had multiple achievements, obstacles, failures and reinventions. I went from making photocopies and designing the first company logo to writing the first manual for consultants and resolving the problems of exponential growth in the early years, and from there to heading up large projects, creating and expanding businesses in Europe, and finally becoming CEO of the company.

I didn't go looking for all this. I simply focused on trying to resolve the huge complexities that I hadn't expected this industry of "conscious consulting" to offer me. It's an industry bursting with enthusiasm, but also vices, clichés, and impulses that were great opportunities for practice.

Now, as a partner and active member of a company that is also a community of people committed to a common purpose, I value the journey even more and I appreciate having been part of something that gave me the chance to meet and work with brilliant people in all their various facets and capacities.

From its inception, Axialent has had the noble purpose of helping people, teams and organizations to express who they want to be in a virtuous way. We do that by working every day to help leaders around the world align the culture of their organizations – and their own behavior – with their business strategies. We have found a way to align intentions with behavior and efficacy.

This journey has also given me the great opportunity of sharing a path with people I admire and from whom I have learned in various ways: Fred Kofman, Carolyn Taylor, Andy Freire, Nithya Shanti, Shauna Shapiro, Jorge Valdano, Bill Withers and Lisa Lahey, to name but a few of the best-known. And, above all, it has afforded me the chance to work shoulder-to-shoulder with many other colleagues and clients who have helped me explore content in depth, looking at new ideas and practices in order to stay abreast of the demands and needs of a changing world that shows no signs of slowing down.

Every year, new trends, fashions and practices arise that present themselves as the perfect solution to all our problems and one which we should all latch onto if we want to stay current. However, I believe that until we develop the capacity to distinguish between that which truly contributes and that which does not, according to who we are and what we want, to value what will work in the long term and what must be tactical, and to differentiate between speed and depth, we will be no more than objects that move without really knowing where we're going – simply pushing forward.

I never intended to write a book about management, life coaching, or leadership. Nor was I looking to write a book of recipes for success or ways to get quick results. This book is an invitation to learn how to learn: something to help us constantly seek the best version of ourselves.

## The four essentials

Everything you will find in the coming pages is based on four axioms which I consider essential. They underpin where I am coming from when I say what I say and suggest what I suggest:

**1.** Our being determines our doing.

**2.** Being alive involves finding new challenges.

**3.** There's always room for improvement.

**4.** Without action, there can be no feedback.

These affirmations, which define how I see life and its challenges, are present throughout the coming chapters and create points of connection between the various topics. And, based on these beliefs, from the very first chapter I propose the following:

There are always new things that we can do in order to express our (next) best version. It's just a matter of focusing.

We often want to bring into practice that virtuous self. There are things we want to change but find it difficult to, and we sometimes wonder why we can't handle it. What ensues is frustration, and we subconsciously enter a vicious cycle that, as we will see, causes our brains and the muscles in our bodies to tense up and become increasingly rigid.

But despite everything, we want to progress. To transform ourselves. To be able to do new things, as sons and daughters, parents, friends, leaders, colleagues, sportspeople or simply by connecting better with others in a world that requires more and more social skills. And this common factor among us all, regardless of our specific country, system, organization or situation, is something permanent. It is a part of being human and part of our daily search.

## So, how do we do this?

This book consists of four parts in which you will find space for reflection and inspiration – for tackling concrete ideas that challenge and invite us to go from ideas to action on the endless learning curve toward the next better version of ourselves.

In the first section, we will look at how the finite nature of life – so often feared and denied – can be a great ally. In the second section, we will look at why we find it so difficult to change, even for the things we really want. In the third section, we will analyze why it's not enough to understand our own individual dynamics and why we must also understand our contexts and the cultures to which we belong. In the fourth and final section, there is a new invitation to call you to action, but you will no longer be the same and you will be able to analyze and act based on new logic.

I must warn you that, one way or another, much of what you will find in these pages will be things you already know, or have heard of, or recognize intuitively. However, you will also likely encounter new ideas and a missing piece of your puzzle. The proposed idea is not so much based on what we don't know as it is on what we need in order to reconnect with things that we *do* know and sense, but have filed away in some corner of our minds.

Each chapter will include case studies, stories and methods from experts with whom I had the pleasure of working and whose practices I have employed with several clients. I propose to show you the various paths that we can take according to who we are, where we are, and what we want. As you will see as you continue to read, I don't believe in a single formula, technique or magic bullet, like so many people would have us believe exists.

I believe in the potential of trying, of learning, and of taking whatever is useful to us depending on our situation and our desires.

## Learning to act: this is the key

We all wish we could rise to challenges in the most virtuous way possible. Like pretty much everyone I know, I want to be the best *me* at all times and in every situation, whether with family, business, the team, my boss, colleagues or when something unexpected happens. We all want to feel proud of ourselves and of how we respond when it comes to "the moment of truth." To do this, we have to evolve and transform something in us in a more profound way. This involves leaving behind deep-seated history, changing any behavior that we're not proud of, or simply developing new skills. In some cases, achieving this is possible – but there are many other situations where it's not that simple, and we often end up throwing in the towel.

This book is for everyone currently on that quest and who constantly second-guesses themselves. For those who feel the need to make a change and grow, and who want to look back on themselves from somewhere else.

Of course, we can't achieve everything we desire. As we will see, results depend on many factors. But learning to act in a different way is within our reach. Finding that version of ourselves that learns from everything and gets better may be the best meta-skill we can develop.

I hope you enjoy the journey. That's my greatest wish. I invite you to be guided by the most relevant question you can ask yourself when faced with anything you decide to invest time, energy and effort in: what do you want to learn? Because seek and you will find.

*Barcelona*
*May 2021*

one

# Finiteness is a virtue

Spirit of my silence, I can hear you.
But I'm afraid to be near you
And I don't know where to begin ...
And we all know how this will end
Chimney swift that finds me,
be my keeper ...
What is that song you sing for the dead?

Sufjan Stevens, "*Death with dignity.*"

**https://spoti.fi/3oQH9Jo**

If you want to listen to the song from the original Spanish version of the book, check it out here

https://spoti.fi/2Tl3cLW

# 1. Choices

I've always been into sports. Don't ask me why – it just happened that way. Maybe my family's values had an impact on it, the school they chose for me, or maybe it was just something I was good at and stood out in.

As a kid I started playing soccer. It was what I most liked to do. I carried a ball with me everywhere! But at home, the family mandate was to study at the Buenos Aires National High School, or *El Colegio*, as its students and alumni tend to call it: a clear indication of the social pedestal it has historically been placed upon. My mom studied there, as did my dad (although only for three years: almost a premonition of the footsteps I would later follow in!), my maternal grandfather, my older sister, my brother... Of course, I was going to go to El Colegio. Ignoring that path wasn't an option. However, in my second year (when I was fourteen), I started trying out in soccer clubs, and the following year – after months of tryouts – I passed all the tests and got to the final selection stage to play in the sixth division of Vélez Sarsfield at a great point in the club's history. It was its golden era, with Carlos Bianchi at the helm and the team winning everything, including the Intercontinental Cup against Milan. The selection process had required me to compete against thousands of other guys and undergo test after test: hundreds of us each time. I could never understand where so many guys I had never seen before were coming from.

With the novelty of all these events, high school was no longer my priority, although I expressed this on a less than conscious level. In the last few weeks of that year – my third of five – I skipped most of my classes and final exams. I prioritized tryouts, training, and getting what I wanted. I'm sure that everything my friends and those who watched me play told me played its part: they saw me as one of the few who could make it. How could I pass up a chance like that, when it was the dream of so many kids like me?

And so, with a confidence that must have surprised her, I told my mom: "I have seven subjects in December. I want to keep studying, but I also want to play soccer, so I think I'm going to change schools." It was clear that I knew that continuing with both highly demanding activities was impossible.

It took years for me to realize that, just as I had gotten into the Buenos Aires National High school on my own merit at twelve years old, I had been able to leave it the same way at fifteen. But it wasn't an easy change at the time, both emotionally and practically speaking. It meant leaving behind tradition: the family mandate. I still remember my mother crying uncontrollably, telling me I was throwing my future down the drain. But I also remember my own anguish when, just a few months later, I injured my knee and wasn't selected at Vélez the following year.

It wasn't until many years later that my brother told me: "You were the first person to break the mandate." Perhaps that was the first step toward making a profound change in my life. I barely realized it, but that change would lead me to experiences that would define me and take me on the path I had decided to travel: challenging what others expected of me and going after what I wanted, even though I knew it would be hard.

## A new world

Playing soccer involved being put to the test virtually every day, at every training session, and taking the constant risk of being excluded. I ended up in a stadium with five thousand other guys to start trials at nine o'clock in the morning, only getting to play at four o'clock in the afternoon, and knowing that ultimately, just a handful – ten or eleven – of us would be chosen.

Then my knee injury happened. Two good friends and I found a new place ten months later in Atlanta, a second-division club. This meant going to the Central Market of Buenos Aires to train. I was sixteen by then, and it was time to make new decisions.

When I left high school and my neighborhood and moved away from my lifelong friends, I found myself in another world – one so different that it changed the way I looked at life. My classmates, fifteen to sixteen years old, often skipped training. I wondered what was wrong with them: what did they have to do that could possibly be more important. And the answer was both simple and devastating: they had to work to maintain their children, or they simply didn't have enough money for the bus. For these guys, the chance to become soccer players was pretty much all they had. That gave me a new outlook on the world. It showed me that universes existed that I didn't know, and it helped me focus even more on what I was doing. It was by chance that I discovered and connected with a reality that I had, so far, been sheltered from.

Every day, I got up at six in the morning and traveled by public transport for an hour and a half to a plot of land to train for five hours. I would study on the bus back, go to my new school in the suburb of Belgrano, and finally come home when it was getting dark outside, knowing that I had given it my all. I had no energy for the things a normal teenager usually does. All I did was sleep, train, eat healthy, study, and repeat. I would fall into bed every night, exhausted.

Sometime later, when my mom saw the effort and discipline that I was putting into the choice I had made, something in her changed, although she didn't tell me about it until many years later. She felt proud; my decision to change schools hadn't been about quitting my studies, or ignoring the values she had instilled in me. It had been about fulfilling my desire to pour all of my energy into something I was passionate about. The effort was the same, it was just the focus that was completely different.

## Death as an advisor

It was then that I learned a huge, early lesson that opened my eyes to how even the best-laid plans can go awry in the blink of an eye. That summer, I went on a trip to Peru with Diego, a close friend from my younger years. The trip showed me a side of the world I had not yet seen, and one which continues to affect me to this day. A few days after we arrived in Lima, we headed for the city of Arequipa for some tourism before going on to Puno and Lake Titicaca. In the middle of the journey, in the black of night, our train stopped for hours with no explanation.

Having spent half the night there, half asleep, we found out we had crashed into a railroad cart: a simple vehicle pushed along the tracks by muscle force, designed to transport rail repairmen.

A near-dead body, wrapped in blankets, was brought aboard our carriage by four people. A mangled leg hung out; the child was screaming in pain.

There had been an entire family traveling on the cart. I heard some passengers – who were almost all locals – mentioning that one member of the family had lost their life, and that another was severely injured. We never found out what happened to them later, but the impact of that incident is still vivid for me. A first impact.

Days later, we went to see the famous Colca Canyon and spent the night in Chivay, a tiny village that lives off tourism. There, the local mini-nightclub (it couldn't have fit more than fifty people inside) was a meeting place for around thirty tourists, including Diego and myself, who were the only people who could speak Spanish. We met Memo, our guide's brother, who was DJing there. We requested a few songs and spent a while chatting about music before going back to sleep, so that we would be well-rested for our visit to the canyon the following day. In the morning, the sky was so overcast that you could barely see the canyon at all. They told us that this was a very common occurrence: something else we hadn't learned until the trip itself. We managed to get a brief look at the beautiful canyon through the cloud cover (and what we couldn't see, we imagined!) and then headed back to Chivay.

When we reached the village, we found out that Memo had died. The minibus he had been driving had overturned in the poor visibility and bad road conditions. I can still remember the reactions of the villagers. It was a scene similar to the one we had witnessed on the train a week before: disbelief, sorrow, but also the sense that these things happen and would go on happening. Unexpected death was part of the fabric of life in those places and for those people. I left convinced that it would happen again soon. I learned to relax, to sleep on the journey back, knowing that I was at the mercy of the driver of our van and that of every driver we crossed during the journey.

That was my first direct connection with the finite nature of life, and it was crude, unexpected, and brutal. It was also a connection to another system of values and beliefs, with cultures and practices that were different from mine. The desire to live hit me like a lightning bolt. The immense sensation that life goes on, that I had another chance, and that the mark we leave behind can take different forms depending on what we choose in each situation.

I was one of the last people to talk to Memo. I was one of the last people he touched with the music he played. The memory of that night made me realize that we never truly know when we are doing something for the last time.

## Changing course

When I got back from Peru, I decided to quit soccer as a professional career (though never as my favorite sport to play) and turn my life around. I felt that I had to go in another direction. As an almost visceral response to everything I had seen and experienced in the last few years, I took up full-time work in the social sector. That's how I found out about the work of *Fundación Iniciativa*, which was in the middle of a revival with just five members. The group was headed up by a brilliant, determined girl, Carola, who led with great professionalism, uniting the past with the present and future and inspiring everyone to do their very best.

The strength of the initiative was its work among the young: people in their late teens promoting projects by fifteen- and sixteen-year-olds. The project amplified people's drive and ideas all over Argentina. I did it for pleasure, and for the challenge of being surrounded by other young people who shared my passion, united by something that brought nothing but positive results. We gave it our all at every moment for those ideas and that group.

Years later, as the foundation grew and Carola left, I became executive director. I felt that I was shouldering a big responsibility, and that was the seed that grew into the work I do today. The job led me to meet people who would go on to shape my adult life, and it was where I learned almost everything I know about leadership, action, teamwork and the importance of making an impact. It was a new turning point: one of those that, when you look back, you see as having a clear before and after.

By twenty-three years old, I was too "old" to carry on at *Iniciativa*, and I realized I had to learn to make myself dispensable, so that my departure wouldn't cause problems for the project. I can't say that I managed it. Years later, the organization was dissolved. The feeling that I was unable to support the new leaders, leave secure structures in place, and – above all – foster a culture that would enable such a noble organization to continue to operate for a long time yet is something that has stayed with me my whole life.

I learned a lot from that experience. Perhaps the most valuable lesson was recognizing that those of us who lead have an impact far beyond the present moment: that we leave a legacy that lasts many years. An equally valuable lesson was that of processing the feeling of having failed at something I felt so strongly about, and I could only fix that by learning something for the future. It always made me feel good to see so many ex-members of *Iniciativa*, as well as participants in its activities, continuing to honor its values. Remembering the time they spent there helps them connect with the best version of themselves. *Iniciativa*'s spirit and purpose live on in every one of those people, and, in that sense, it is eternal.

## The path to acceptance

While I was completing my course in Institutional Management and Organization, having spent three years studying Sociology, I began work as a consultant for big companies on the topic of social responsibility. The job was offered to me by a great teacher, and one who is now my friend and travel buddy, Félix Bombarolo. He invited me to be a part of his projects and to learn by working alongside him. And so, two worlds – business and social – came together.

One year and some months later, I received a call that opened the doors to a new project, as yet unnamed. It aimed to help leaders with high impact within their organizations to work more consciously, humanely and effectively. This was the beginning of Axialent.

Since 2002, Axialent has afforded me the opportunity to work with thousands of leaders from all over the world. I have been able to help them lead their teams better, take on complex situations with composure and resilience, and in many cases effect great cultural change within their organizations and themselves. Each of these experiences served to help me with the next. In addition, being able to accompany others has been the best incentive and inspiration in my own life journey.

As Fred Kofman, founder of Axialent and a great teacher, would say: "To scuba dive ten meters underwater with our clients, we need to be able to go fifty meters deep by ourselves, to know how it feels to be there." That's what we did when we trained with him, doing things we could never have imagined.

I remember one retreat in particular. We called it "Samurai Week." At one point, we were doing a trust exercise – one with a lot of masculine energy. It involved forcing those present to rank each other according to whom they would trust most in an extreme life-threatening situation. I remember that Fred – who, to my great pride, placed me in his top three – told me "To trust you more in extreme situations, I'd like to see more of your dark side." I naively and unthinkingly rebutted the idea, to which Fred replied: "I don't think you know what your dark side is. Tomorrow, we're going to do an exercise so that you can all connect with yours."

The following day, he took us to an area away from the resort. In the middle of the countryside, far away from the hotel in a wooded area, we participated in an activity in which I felt and experienced something I had never connected with before, though it had always been there: my capacity to cause harm, to hurt people.

The exercise consisted of telling someone in the group something that we believed was the worst thing someone could do to us, and what would bring out the worst in us: rage, anger, belligerence. Three or four people in the group would then form a squad to hold back our anger: someone would tell you to your face the worst thing they could think of, and the rest would hold you back in every possible way, to make you feel powerless.

Pablo went first. Innocently, he stated that the worst thing that could happen to him would be that his son would be kidnapped. I witnessed his face, with a playful smile on it at the beginning, transform over the course of the exercise, becoming shaken and distressed. He became someone capable of shaking off four of his colleagues from holding him back, swinging wildly for the person telling him he had his son and intended to hurt him badly.

Then, it was my turn. After three minutes of listening to two people repeat the name of my then-partner and tell me the things they would do to her, it got real. I couldn't shake off the arms of those holding me back against my will, but that didn't stop me feeling that I needed to hurt the people speaking, needed to stop them. In that moment, I felt the true desire to destroy another person.

I know many people will not like this. I don't even know if I would do it today. In that context, it was perfect – at that moment, in that place and with those people. It was definitely helpful for me. Despite the violence you might read into this story, it all took place in a carefully controlled environment.

The value of this exercise lay in how it connected me with a part of myself that had been hidden, but that was there, expressing itself in other ways. That physical and emotional connection with my capacity to do harm has stayed with me in every relationship, helping me to see a part of myself that I had concealed even from myself. It was the first time I was able to connect with the depth that it takes to ask for forgiveness when we hurt others.

Through what Fred gave us with that exercise and many of the activities we did, I learned that having experiences is one of the best ways to learn and get to know ourselves. It's not about talking – it's about doing. And leadership is not a path you can follow from a map. Leadership means having the chance to inspire others and help them find the best version of themselves by offering them experiences and the right context for them. It is the ability to listen and connect, in any situation, with those around us but also with our own fears and desires. It means giving encouragement, saying those words that can move mountains, as well as respecting life's little silences. It means understanding that there are as many paths as there are ways to travel them.

That's what exploring is about: accepting what we don't know and deciding to learn. Life is finite, and you only live once, but there are infinite ways to do it.

# 2. The eternal search for meaning

The story of Memo, on that trip to Peru with its experiences and deaths, made me wonder about the meaning of life. I don't mean the existential question of what we are doing here, but something more mundane, like simply knowing what we want to do in life. That question, which I asked myself so many times, always brought me back to the same notion: we all lose life's final battle. Whether we like it or not. Sooner or later, we all die. And before that inevitable end, we will fight hundreds of little battles that we cannot lose, or so we believe.

We cling to near-divine ideas about what is supposedly good and bad, and we turn success into a mantra: everything has to work out the way we think it should – or how others say it should – and we pour endless amounts of time and energy into making this happen. It's as if life were a race, and we try to deny even the most overwhelming facts life presents us with, from the uncertainty of our path to the certainty of our demise.

My proposal is to try something different:

We can choose to live this journey, and the time that we have, as a continuous learning opportunity that deserves to be experienced.

Wouldn't it help us to look at the horizon more often, connect with our finiteness and our fragility, acknowledge our limitations, gain humility and actively pick only some of those "battles" that we fight every day, to experience them from another perspective?

Let's be honest: apart from a minute number of exceptions, a hundred years from now, no one will remember that tense conversation we had this morning with our boss, or the business decision we made last week having tried to convince everyone we were right. The organizations we work for probably won't even exist: the companies where we fight so hard to beat our competitors and be the best in the market.

It is highly unlikely that everything we attach so much importance to in our daily lives will ever be remembered: our organizations, our decisions, the way we mull over situations in our minds, dedicating more hours to them than we would like to. However, we do all this with an extraordinary amount of intensity and dedication, tremendously keen to win every argument, to be right and to come across as perfect, successful, near invincible. As if we don't know, deep down, that this too shall pass.

This is not an invitation to complacency or to extreme hedonism. This doesn't mean you shouldn't give your all. Quite the opposite! Giving your all is much easier when you can connect with the best version of yourself, the most virtuous you. The one who does things and produces things out of the pleasure and commitment of adding value, not out of the need to win battles.

Who do I want to be when life presents me with my next challenge? What would make me proud to say and do if this were the last conversation we were to have? These questions are an invitation to put all your energy into that which you can control: into living, leading, sharing and being a part of everything you do, aligned with anything that helps make you the best version of yourself.

I know that what I am suggesting may be difficult. It seems that way from the viewpoint we construct for ourselves: as if we have to leave everything for "later" because now is the time to enjoy ourselves, to accumulate stuff, to achieve. But who really knows if they have a "later"? So, what happens if we change the way we look at things?

The question, then, is *who do I want to be* in the face of each challenge, and *how do I want to do it*. The answer won't be in the objective, but in how we live, think and act in order to make this happen. It is in how our intentions become actions.

## Who I want to be

I remember a long chat with Nithya Shanti, not long after I met him. He had recently left the Buddhist monastery in Thailand where he had spent seven years, and a mutual friend introduced us, thinking we might be able to do good things together. And we did. Now, not only do we do things together for clients, but I consider him a great mentor, friend and travel companion.

During one of our first talks, he told me that he was very clear on three intentions that guided him and enabled him to see himself, reflect, and improve at the service of what he was seeking in life. This is what has made him a source of inspiration, connection and learning for thousands upon thousands of people.

The three intentions that he shared with me during that chat (and which can be found online by searching "Nithya Shanti power of intentions") are as follows:

**To learn:** to always do things in order to keep on learning.

**To practice what I learn:** what I learn only makes sense if I practice and apply it.

**To share:** I want to expand what I practice and value by sharing it with others.

According to Nithya, this turns everything into a virtuous cycle: "When I share, I learn, and when I practice, I integrate, which makes it easier to share. I don't want to see myself, nor for others to see me, as an expert, but rather as someone who always keeps an open mind and is a learner."

Nithya is successful at what he does because he focuses on what he is passionate about and on how he does that, which in turn becomes the best he can offer the world, and the world rewards him for that.

After I listened to him, many of the things I had been working on more or less fell into place on their own. Firstly, understanding the power of intentions rather than having expectations, which involves hoping for things from others, including positive feedback and results. This enables us to focus our energy on what each of us can do to honor the way we want to respond to every event. The impact we have on others is valuable information, not to make us feel guilty but to help us decide what we want to do with it.

I myself defined three intentions which I still hold today:

---

**To consciously connect:** To be one hundred per cent present in what I'm doing, here and now. With myself, with what I feel and think. And with others when they are with me.

---

**To generously support:** Every connection is an opportunity to help someone achieve the best version of themselves.

---

**To kindly challenge:** Reflect effectively the inconsistencies between what we say we want to be and what we are actually able to do.

---

## The placebo of unconsciousness

Often when I talk to clients or colleagues, I realize not many of them are clear on what their intentions are. They really have to think about it, and their answers are still vague. It's as if it were better to leave some things undecided. But why do that with something so central to our lives?

There are some advantages to not delving too deep into questions for which we have no answer. What is the meaning of life, how do we want to live, what do we want to leave behind: these are uncomfortable questions, and we don't always like to ask them. Our finiteness and our vulnerability are topics we don't like to touch upon unless absolutely necessary.

Many will remember the movie *The Matrix* (1999, Lana and Lilly Wachowski) and in particular one of its most troubling scenes: when Morpheus, played by Laurence Fishburne, reveals to Keanu Reeves' hacker Neo that everything he sees around him is part of a fabricated reality. He offers him a dilemma: stay in the Matrix, with no awareness of what he has just been told, or disconnect from that automatic life and start living in "the real world."

---

**Morpheus:** The Matrix is everywhere. It is all around us. Even now, in this very room. You can see it when you look out your window, or when you turn on your television. You can feel it when you go to work, when you go to church, when you pay your taxes. It is the world that has been pulled over your eyes to blind you from the truth.

**Neo:** What truth?

**Morpheus:** That you are a slave, Neo. Like everyone else you were born into bondage. Born into a prison that you cannot smell or taste or touch. A prison for your mind. Unfortunately, no one can be told what the Matrix is. You have to see it for yourself. This is your last chance. After this, there is no turning back. You take the blue pill, the story ends: you wake up in your bed and believe whatever you want to believe. You take the red pill, you stay in Wonderland and I show you how deep the rabbit hole goes. Remember: all I'm offering is the truth. Nothing more.

---

*The Matrix* functions as a metaphor for how far we are prepared to open our eyes at any given moment. To feel what we feel. To reflect on that degree of unconsciousness that enables us to live day-to-day without the burden of contemplating the irrefutable truth. But even if we shy away from it, sooner or later, life will take us to that place. Reality and all its perceptions will get us in the end.

When we least expect it, something affects us so deeply that it reminds us we are not eternal. That's what happened to me on that trip to Peru, or it happens with the loss of a loved one, like when my paternal grandmother died. A global crisis, like the pandemic that began in 2020. Or any other extreme situation that befalls us and gives us a dose of reality.

Suddenly, we find ourselves looking at our lives from the outside, wondering about all the things we don't want to think about, trying to understand how we got where we are, and sometimes realizing we don't know how we got here, much less what our next step will be.

Just a few months ago, a colleague told me that a close friend of his had been diagnosed with a very aggressive type of cancer. He knew his friend was going to die soon. That moment of awareness had thrown his own life into perspective. But he also told me that he knew from previous, similar situations that after a while, he would get used to the new situation and everything would go back to more or less how it was before.

Death makes us so uneasy that we forget it exists. Until it bursts into our lives and gives us a moment of wake-up call, that is.

Fear of death follows
from the fear of life.
A man who lives fully
is prepared to die
at any time.

Mark Twain

## Something to believe in

Life delivers blows that lead us to think the unthinkable, to put into words things we had been refusing to say, to give us ideas that might seem rash: None of this has any clear meaning. It only has the meaning we give it.

That seems to be the big question: Why do we do what we do? What is the meaning of being alive, here and now?

Some people believe in a god or a destiny; others believe in biology and free will. We choose certain ideas depending on our beliefs, and cling to them as if they were objective truths. But the truth is that we don't really know what life is about. Every one of us chooses stories, tales, and interpretations to give life some meaning. Science helps us to explain it in one way, philosophy in another; psychoanalysis plays a part, and, of course, there are religions, which have been creating stories about the human condition since time immemorial.

As Yuval Noah Harari explains in his book *Sapiens: A Brief History of Humankind* (2011), these tales are the main reason why we have prevailed over all other species: we have a unique quality. So, what is that quality?

It is the ability to form groups and cooperate in order to achieve a purpose impossible for an individual.

As individuals, humans are no more sophisticated or more capable than most other species. If you put one of us along with a chimpanzee on a desert island, the chimp would probably win out and live longer than any one person. But what if you put a hundred chimpanzees and a hundred *Homo sapiens*? The outlook would be very different, because we humans have the capacity to join forces and commit to an idea, cause, or meaning. That is the story of humanity. Our story. That is what gets us out of bed every morning and makes us feel that we are part of something bigger than ourselves, even if that something is a work of fiction constructed centuries ago and in which we choose to continue believing, precisely because it helps us find meaning in what we do.

Harari says: "How exactly did Armand Peugeot, the man, create Peugeot, the company? In much the same way that priests and sorcerers have created gods and demons throughout history, [...] It all revolved around telling stories, and convincing people to believe them. [...] Much of history revolves around this question: How does one convince millions of people to believe particular stories about gods, or nations, or limited liability companies? Yet when it succeeds, it gives Sapiens immense power, because it enables millions of strangers to cooperate and work towards common goals. Just try to imagine how difficult it would have been to create states, or churches, or legal systems if we could speak only about things that really exist, such as rivers, trees and lions."

So, is there some transcendental meaning behind these stories we tell ourselves? I believe there are as many purposes as there are human beings. Thinking about what gives us meaning, along with our intentions, can help us to understand that the things we want to change, learn, or improve only make sense and serve us when they are aligned with our purpose, aspirations and desires.

## From "stories" to "our story"

Life is also about acquiring the ability to live peacefully with all its dualities and be able to integrate them. It's about being open to challenging and questioning ourselves. Being able to grow and acknowledge new evidence and beliefs. Accepting that there are ideas and emotions that are in opposition to each other while still being true, and living with them as long as it takes to really decide.

Many of our daily problems, as well as our difficulties in expressing the best versions of ourselves, arise because we disconnect from anything that is painful for us without stopping to wonder if those parts of life aren't what lend meaning to the things that we *do* want and yearn for. Without stopping to wonder if, perhaps, the sum of all those parts is what shapes who we are today.

Viktor Frankl was an Austrian neurologist, psychiatrist and philosopher, and the founder of logotherapy. By the time he did so, he had survived four Nazi concentration camps – including Auschwitz – between 1942 and 1945. One of his best-known books, entitled *Man's Search for Meaning,* was published shortly after the end of World War Two. In the preface, Gordon W. Allport ponders: "His father, mother, brother, and his wife died in camps or were sent to the gas ovens, so that, excepting for his sister, his entire family perished in these camps. How could he – every possession lost, every value destroyed, suffering from hunger, cold and brutality, hourly expecting extermination – how could he find life worth preserving?"

And while Frankl's book is worth reading, I can tell you now that the answer is short and simple: "When we are no longer able to change a situation, we are challenged to change ourselves. [...] We who lived in concentration camps can remember the men who walked through the huts comforting others, giving away their last piece of bread. They may have been few in number, but they offer sufficient proof that everything can be taken from a man but one thing: the last of the human freedoms – to choose one's attitude in any given set of circumstances, to choose one's own way."

The best way we can learn from our experiences – even from those that have caused us pain – is by connecting with the apparently contradictory emotions they throw up. The paradox of this is that we must develop the ability to recognize value and to try to be grateful for – or at least appreciate the contribution of – everything that happens to us, even if it seems difficult at the time.

And I'm not talking about resignation. I'm not talking about accepting things without deciding how we want to respond. I'm talking about being able to accept that everything that has happened has made us who we are right now. It has been part of the fabric of our stories and brought us here, now, today, reading these pages. Everything so far has been the summation of countless turning points that we can connect together if we stop to think about it. And if we stop for a few seconds and breathe, we realize that, in this place, at this very moment, everything is perfect.

# 3. Where is the best version of ourselves?

## The mantra that doesn't work

"Health, wealth and love" is a mantra that supposedly sums up everything we need in life. Almost all of us want – or say we want – the same thing: to be happy. And we often say that "success" in life means simply being happy. I have my doubts regarding what this means for each individual person. But first, let us look at what Harari has to say about this so-called "universal truth": "The most important finding of all is that happiness does not really depend on objective conditions of either health, wealth or even community. Rather, it depends on the correlation between objective conditions and subjective expectations. If you want a bullock-cart and get a bullock-cart, you are content. If you want a brand-new Ferrari and get only a second-hand Fiat, you feel deprived. [...] When things improve, expectations balloon, and consequently even dramatic improvements in objective conditions can leave us dissatisfied. [...] If happiness depended only on objective conditions such as wealth, health and social relations, it would have been relatively easy to investigate its history. The finding that it depends on subjective expectations makes the task of historians far harder."

It is possible that, on the one hand, many of us know many healthy, wealthy people in relationships and with beautiful families who, despite all that, still feel unhappy and question themselves, wondering why they are not happy when they have everything that other human beings could want. On the other hand, it is possible that we also know people who have much less than all of that and yet feel fulfilled, inspired and altogether happy. So, how does this work?

Nithya Shanti categorizes four types of happiness that we can experience. Whenever I share them with people, they serve as a source of constructive reflection for understanding the place from which we do the things we do. That's why I asked him to write them down so I could share them in this book. I hope you find them to be as much of a revelation as I did, and that they help you to understand the ways in which you can choose to live each day.

## Four Kinds of Happiness

*by Nithya Shanti*

*In my journey I realized that there are broadly four kinds of happiness. Let me explain each of these...*

**No Happiness:** This is when we focus on what is wrong or missing in our life. This is also when we overtly or covertly complain, compare and fault-find. This is the state of being a victim. We feel weak and disempowered. Our mind is saturated with thoughts of what has been wrong, is wrong and can go wrong in our life. We tend to be reactive, impulsive and fixated on short term distractions. Emotions associated with such a state are guilt, resentment, fear, anxiety, helplessness. The belief is that everything is imperfect and getting worse. However, it is also the rich soil from which the tree of the other kinds of happiness can blossom if met with acceptance and understanding.

**Happiness for the Wrong Reason:** This is an "outside-in" approach to happiness. The happiness of events going our way. When we fall for the twin myths of "more" and "when," it tends to be happiness for the wrong reason. "More" implies more money, time, opportunities, etc. will finally make us happy. "When" implies once loans are paid off, education is complete, kids grow up, etc. it will finally make us happy. This is the tendency to postpone happiness to the end point of some imagined ideal situation. While we can be more active, engaged and energetic in this state than in the previous one, it is often based on pursuing things that we have been told or conditioned to want. Emotions associated with this state include pride, frustration, anger, attachment, a sense of urgency and not enough time, restlessness, excitement followed by disappointment. The belief is that things are imperfect and hopefully will get better sometime in the future. Often people do a lot and even outwardly accomplish a lot in this state. Yet it does not usually satisfy and fulfill them in ways they had hoped it would.

**Happiness for a Good Reason:** This is the blameless happiness of enjoying the process no less than the outcome. So instead of doing things for joy, we do them with joy. Instead of doing things for peace, we do them from peace, with peace, as peace. The recognition that what we are really seeking is a state of being more than any specific outcome is strong here. It is an "inside-out" form of happiness. Taking a walk in nature, spending time with close friends, enjoying a hobby, preparing a wholesome meal are some examples where many people experience this form of happiness. However, it is not limited to any such activities. Whenever we have the attitude "what can I bring to this" instead of "what can I get from this," we are happy for a good reason. Feelings associated with this state are: acceptance, gratitude, contentment, compassion, grace, lightness and fulfillment. The belief is that everything is perfect and keeps getting better. There is the trust that whatever will be, will be.

**Happiness for No Reason:** This is the shift from person to presence. When we no longer feel "we are living a life," instead we realize we are "life living life." We do not feel we are moving through the world, it appears like the world moving through and around us, as we remain the silent witness. Every moment is complete. Every place is sacred. Every meeting is a holy encounter with another aspect of ourself. We have a sense of being awake within a dream, a dream that is without a dreamer. We approach life with few if any agendas and presumptions. There is spontaneous innocence accompanied with an uncontrived depth and wisdom in everything we do. We are no longer trying to please others, we express our truth authentically yet don't place ourselves in opposition to anyone or anything. In this state there is transparency, spaciousness, ease, bliss of being, flow, joy without an enjoyer, peace without a center. The attitude is that everything is in the right place. We realize that it takes something to be unhappy and it takes nothing to be happy. We embrace all of ourselves and all of life as it presents itself without resistance, calculation or manipulation. We do not "get this state of being," this state of being "gets us," the part of us that assumed it was controlling the flow of life. There is sweet relief and immaculate freedom.

*We can travel between these four kinds of happiness multiple times each day. We can spend as much or as little time in any of these states. In a sense the quality of our life is determined by which state we spend the most time in, (although in the last state even time is does not limit or constrain us). We can only inhabit one state at a time, though it is possible to oscillate between them frequently. The one we visit most frequently, begins to feel like home.*

## In search of happiness

When we dare to think about life and death, and the ways in which our awareness of them impacts on our decisions, the following ideas emerge: counting on others, helping those in need, connecting with people we love, making a difference in the world (or in *our* world). Every religion shares similar notions, just in different styles and with their own individual nuances.

Every day, we humans live with this matter which is almost inherent to our condition; it is the feeling of success if we manage to transcend. That is why we have children, differentiate ourselves from other species through our concepts of past and future, and seek to leave behind a legacy.

However, many of our everyday actions are not necessarily aligned with what brings us the most fulfilment and happiness. Daily life throws up more "urgent" matters that we have to prioritize, and we tend to believe that everything else can wait, that we have time, that we will find space for what's important later. And so, our mind fools itself and fools us, as if all of those *extremely* urgent things were definitive.

In a conversation aimed at designing a session for a team of leaders, Nithya shared with me a definition that really influenced the way I look at what it is that makes us feel that fulfilment at all times, without expecting to obtain anything concrete. He mentioned five qualities that help him feel he is living life to the full.

---

Being present.

---

Connecting with love and compassion.

---

Being grateful for everything.

---

Expressing joy.

---

And learning to "let go."

---

Over the next few days, as I went over his words in my head, I once again realized that profound happiness can never depend on an outcome. We are far more likely to find happiness when we develop the ability to live more and more in the present moment. The here and now. Feeling what we feel. Thinking what we think. Being with whom we are with. And every situation is an opportunity to experiment with how to do it. Not only do we get better when we go through those moments of great transformation over the course of our lives, but also when we consciously go through those tiny, continuous micro-changes that we can experience in everyday situations.

A successful life can't be defined by certifications or exams, nor by measuring fortune and material wealth. All of this can help – it can even be an expression of the path we have traveled, and it's healthy to celebrate it. But on its own, it can also be a new source of frustration. Why? Because it can foster in us the need for more and more achievements of that kind as if they were goals in themselves, and we can forget the true reasons that inspired them.

Beyond what we do, beyond the tangible things we achieve, the momentary wins throughout our lives, careers and professions, the fundamental condiment we all need is the sensation that we belong, that we are part of something, along with others. That is the ability to connect. It's what we feel every time we take on a new challenge with a trusting bond with those we interact with, and the personal feeling of being aligned and connected with our values.

## Reconnecting

Since 1938 (that is, over the course of eight decades), the Harvard Study of Adult Development conducted research into the lives of over seven hundred men. It involved asking them about their family lives, homes, health and desires, year after year. In a TED Talk, American psychiatrist Robert J. Waldinger revealed that around 60 of the 724 men who began the study in 1938 were still alive and active within the study, and that he had begun to trace around two thousand children of the experiment's original participants.

Waldinger, the fourth director of the study, summed up in that talk the main three findings of the study:

---

**First finding:** Social connections are good for us, and loneliness kills. People with more social links to family, friends, and the community are happier and healthier and live longer than people with fewer links. Loneliness is toxic.

---

**Second finding:** Quality is important. Well-being is not related to the number of friends one has, or whether or not one is in a romantic relationship. What is important is the quality of one's closest relationships.

---

**Third finding:** Good relationships protect not just the body, but the brain, too. This was confirmed through many cases in which an environment consisting of good relationships preserved the memories of people over eighty, while people less well-protected in their surroundings were clearly more prone to memory loss.

---

He ventured a disruptive conclusion: What did we learn? Well, the lessons were not related to wealth, fame or hard work. The clearest message of these decades of research was that good relationships make us happier and healthier. Period.

For that reason, *connection* is an important term in our field. Of course, I'm not talking about getting online – in these Covid-19 times, we are hyper-connected but unable to hug other people or feel their warmth – but rather about getting in touch with what's important to us, and what others say is important to them, without judging either ourselves or other people.

So why do we disconnect from ourselves and those around us? Much of this disconnect occurs because we are constantly making value judgements about what is happening around us: what is good and what is bad, whether or not we like something someone did or said. We place people – and ourselves – on what we believe to be the correct or incorrect side of things, depending on the standards they meet or don't meet. Instead of being aware of our own needs and those of others, of the ways to help them and ourselves beat the loneliness we tend to feel when we only listen to our own minds, we simply have a conversation with ourselves and our own standards. This is how it is possible for us to be surrounded by people and still be completely alone. We only listen to ourselves and our own egos, and they take over our minds.

Pay attention to what you're thinking about right now. Or try the same thing during a mundane conversation at home or work.

Who are you listening to?

## The teachings of Tiziano

Tiziano Terzani was born in Florence in 1938. He had a long career as a reporter and war correspondent, retired in 1997 and spent a large portion of his final years in the Himalayas before dying in 2004 at the age of sixty-five. His work has been compiled in various books – many of them relating to his travels as a correspondent in Asia, where he was the first foreigner to cover the war in Mao's China. He bids farewell to us in *The End is My Beginning* (2006), a moving book made up of conversations with his son Folco while he tried to die in peace at his wife's side in his home in Tuscany. It condenses the great lessons learned in a life characterized by travel, places, cultures and people: the importance of genuine connections with other people.

Having traveled the world, seen wars, been a fervent communist and reaped nothing but disappointment from that and every other political and economic organization he came into contact with, Terzani reached the conclusion that what is truly important in life is the ability not to judge, to connect with others, to help them do what they want to in a better way:

> One can get out of the trance by making a witty comment, but, deep down, giving an answer is much more difficult (...) If you ask me what I leave at the end, I leave a book that can perhaps help someone to see the world in a better way to enjoy their own life more, to see it in a broader context [...] We must use the discovery of not being the body, of not being your identity, your books, but being part of something else that is indifferent to all that, and that perhaps one day that can help man find a path. [...] To the young people who ask me, "What do I do?" I answer, "Look! The world is full of things to explore."

Explore and learn. Get out of the inertia. Avoid judgements. Connect with others and be diverse. Find out about others' stories and beliefs.

Life is not a puzzle we can solve once and for all. The meaning of this journey is more like a kaleidoscope, full of shapes and colors that combine and change as we move it. The more we dare to experiment, the more we doubt those so-called objective truths that we order our lives around, the closer we get to understanding what makes us who we are. This enables us to create spaces where we can align what we do with what we want, and find people who can – and want to – be part of this journey with us.

## The various versions of ourselves

We exist within that kaleidoscope, with all its range of colors. We are not just one person – we are myriad versions of ourselves depending on context, on the people around us, even on whether or not the sun is shining that day.

How many times, in various situations, have we questioned whether we are truly being ourselves, as if there were some unchanging nucleus we move away from or get closer to depending on what we do? It is rare for any of us to be the same person all the time, regardless of where we are or what we are doing. It would be like clinging to rigidity: this is me, like it or lump it, take it or leave it.

I believe there are many versions of oneself. Or, more accurately, a single version that expresses itself in different ways. The same essence, fears, aspirations, and beliefs, perhaps, but conveyed in different ways depending on the context. As we will see later on, culture and sub-culture influence these contexts. Some help us to express ourselves in a way more closely aligned with our values, and some do the opposite. But much of what brings us closer to the best of all of those versions lies in being consciously connected to what we think, believe and do.

That best version enables us to express in a virtuous way everything we believe, as well as cutting down recovery times when we don't achieve something. Often, all we can do is acknowledge that something is out of alignment and decide what to do in order to realign it. We will never be perfect, but we can always act in ways more closely aligned with our intentions.

We can always do something to recenter ourselves. That may just be the greatest skill we can develop in order to fall into the virtuous cycle we seek. For this, it is fundamental to implement practices that connect us with the best of our intentions and with the things that make us feel profoundly fulfilled.

When we fully accept the finite nature of everything around us, we have the chance opportunity to utilize every situation in order to practice the best version of ourselves. To learn. To change, to progress, to transform. And that chance opportunity is always now: at the precise moment at which we acknowledge it.

two

# There is an art to change
(and a trick to it)

I watch the ripples change their size
But never leave the stream of warm
impermanence and so the days flow
through my eyes...

DAVID BOWIE, "*Changes.*"

**https://spoti.fi/3crBm7f**

If you want to listen
to the song from
the original Spanish
version of the book,
check it out here

https://spoti.fi/3c1fhMH

# 4. Changing the way we change

Ever since I was little, I have always talked a lot. I like to transmit things through words. To converse. I'm used to doing it, and I always thought: "That's me, this is how I am." It's the story I told myself in order not to have to reflect on something that was right under my nose: people telling me I didn't listen attentively, that I interrupted others or that I appeared not to care what others were saying because I was too absorbed in my own ideas. What could I do? And then, in 2005, a series of events led me to decide to take a vow of silence.

Axialent was in its infancy. At twenty-six, I was the youngest and most inexperienced of the group of consultants, trained under the leadership of Fred Kofman. Given my role as a member of management staff, I had never before considered working directly with clients. I didn't think there were any real obstacles to my getting along with people, either. But that changed. During a retreat in Tilcara, Jujuy, in northwestern Argentina, I felt profoundly challenged. Faced with the beautiful Cerro de los Siete Colores (the hill of the seven colors), surrounded by the immensity of the mountains, nature and a deep appreciation of silence, I was struck by something: there was a great external silence, but I could not quiet my mind.

We spent five days there, removed from daily life, with the aim of working on our desires, strengths and weaknesses. The idea was to connect with ourselves and improve as a team in order to work better with clients and colleagues. In one of the many moments of conscious breathing and introspection, I realized that I had never before experienced that kind of silence: the kind that calms your mind. I could not silence myself internally. Until then, I had never accessed my deepest thoughts or emotions. What was making it so difficult to access a new ability? The fact that I was doing well. I was recognized for my leadership, I formed part of a successful team, so why change? That is one of the greatest inhibitors to change.

That retreat was the perfect place to explore the reasons why I should change. At Axialent, not only was the capacity to reflect valued highly, but also the ability to take risks, experiment, make mistakes and learn lessons from each attempt to do something new. The company I was helping to develop presented me with a personal challenge: Could I turn myself into someone who could relate professionally to colleagues and clients from a different place? Could I integrate something new? Was I capable of growing and developing skills to become a better leader, a better member of the team, and more effective in every aspect of my life?

At that point, I was not fully aware of the magnitude of this challenge. For over twenty-six years, I had learned that talking , directing, and telling people what to do worked well for me. But there was something whispering to me when I listened to myself. That is why I decided to take that challenge to the extreme. Knowing the extremes of something helps me to choose my own center and balance. To be able to integrate it. Trying ten per cent of something usually doesn't offer us a proper experience. Bearing that in mind, I took a vow of silence. I would not speak for three days, to see what happened, how I felt, what new space I might access.

And what was the outcome? It was one of the best experiences of my life. Of course, it wasn't easy. It was an experience that took me out of my comfort zone and enabled me to learn from myself, to learn from skills my mind didn't know I had, and – above all – to learn from other people. Almost for the first time, I managed to truly listen to others.

Little by little, with no words with which to articulate my ideas, my thoughts cleaned themselves up and I began to pay more attention to other people. For the first time, I felt reduced interference in my mind, and I realized I wanted to listen rather than simply needing to give a response. It was a transformational exercise for me, and I learned to figure out when it was my turn to say something and when it was time to listen. For seventy-two hours, I listened to others, and nothing more. Understanding their emotions through registering the tones of their voices, their expressions, and their gestures. Simply listening, without needing to say anything at all.

But if you think the challenge ended there, you're wrong. I had imposed a rule upon myself, and I was following it to the letter. The true challenge came when the self-imposed rule expired, and I was once again "free" to talk. Without the restrictions of the vow of silence, the moment of truth had arrived.

I was learning to connect: to listen to others with no regard for my own story. To accept the other person's story without constantly filtering it through the prism of my own beliefs and biases. To bear in mind that we don't see the world as it is – we see it as we are. It was time to turn what I had achieved in my experiment into a habit.

## Understanding versus being capable

Today, we talk about change, progress and transformation in almost every field imaginable. For me, it's cause for celebration that something so good for us has become a trend. But trends are changeable and fleeting, so I would prefer for some habits to become more conscious: a new way of doing things and an integral part of who we are.

There is a lot of confusion surrounding this "trend"; it is not always clear what change is or what it involves. Repeating it out loud like a mantra doesn't help us to understand it any better. In fact, it can even make us feel frustrated at times: we feel that we should know it, we should do it, we should understand it – but we can't always do that. We tend to assume that a simple idea will be enough to modify our behavior or those of the people around us. Hearing something that we like or that challenges us convinces our minds that we are capable of putting it into practice without considering the enormous effort it may require. The idea of effortlessly changing to obtain what we most want is a common pitfall. This mostly occurs when we think about ourselves, but also when we project onto other people. It can be easier to see the things that are difficult to change when we translate it to other people.

I want to be very clear and direct about this: understanding something conceptually is not sufficient to learn how to do it.

If we knew how to do it, we wouldn't need to learn it – we probably wouldn't even need to think about it. We would already be doing it!

In all my years of work with leaders and teams, I have come across countless examples of people and systems (teams, organizations, and so on) who claimed to *know* something – even to be passionate about it and consider it key to their futures – while being incapable of putting it into practice in the way they want or as quickly or effectively as they want. I have also met many people who managed to achieve significant changes, but abandoned them at the first hurdle, scurrying back to shelter in their old habits and behaviors. I have also seen people who successfully got on the path of profound, sustainable change, with lasting effects in their personal, professional and cultural lives.

What enables us to learn new ways of doing things and to make them part of who we are? We will talk about these difficulties and how to overcome them over the next few pages.

Understanding something is not the same as knowing how to do it. Learning happens when we make it part of our lives.

Those of you reading this book can probably identify many concrete examples – from your own experience or other people's – of this discrepancy between conceptually understanding something and doing or transforming it. The question is what we do about it now, tomorrow, and when we once again realize that we are not talking merely about the people around us, but about ourselves, too.

Concepts are necessary ideas to help our brains connect with our bodies and enable us to find meaning in our efforts. But just because those ideas are necessary does not mean they are enough by themselves. Just look at some simple, everyday situations in your own life: Who would you trust to take care of a small child in a swimming pool for the first time? Someone who has read the best books on how to be a good swimmer, instructor and lifeguard, and who could recite every technique in existence but has only been in the water a handful of times in their life? Or someone who can't read and has no access to modern technology, but who has been swimming and saving people from the water for years? The answer is obvious, especially when we're talking life or death. But something leads us to believe that our own learning processes operate on a different plane: for us, and the people in our ecosystems, it is enough to know how to do something in order to do it. We somehow imagine that rationally understanding how to do something gives us a greater ability to actually do it, so we spend hours listening to talks, reading articles and talking about what we have seen and *understand* like the backs of our hands.

## "But... we already know this!"

Perhaps that is why the first reaction I tend to encounter among the leaders I work with is "We've already studied that," or "I read that book already," or "teach us something new, something we don't know." And I just smile; if they really knew it already, we wouldn't be there, about to start working on it. They may know these things on an intellectual and rational level, but – as we have seen – that doesn't mean that they can *do* it.

The more intellectually intelligent people are, the greater their risk of believing in their own story and clinging to it. In my line of work, I come across people I consider to be highly intelligent every day. People who challenge me. People whose virtues I admire. This happens because, generally speaking, the organizations I work with contain people highly trained in the art of conversation, discussion and negotiation. The problem is that said conversation devolves into an endless stream of conceptual arguments that work as a placebo for action.

## The risk of creating antibodies

When projects for change involve long training processes but don't achieve the desired results, they evoke a reaction that makes the transformation task even more difficult: frustration. Talking about change, trying to bring it about, and failing to do so generates antibodies. It causes *immunity to change*.

We believe that it is enough to want to do it and to convince others. As a result, we don't pay enough mind to the fact that, generally speaking, we lack the right plan, persistence and patience to bring about effective change. It's a pretty simple equation: we overestimate our ability to incorporate new ways of doing things and underestimate the effort necessary to implement new habits and practices.

Experience, however, indicates quite the opposite: the vast majority of the time, change involves leaving intellect aside and making an effort, with all of our senses, to question the ideas and habits that we have incorporated on autopilot. Our mind resists the unknown and anything that takes effort. It reminds us that the ideas and habits we are trying to quit have worked at other times, and it whispers in our ear that getting rid of them could place us at risk.

## 66 days!

James Clear, author of *Atomic Habits*, says that in order for a change to become a sustainable habit – a new way of doing things – it takes around sixty-six days on average, depending on the nature of the habit. Until that timeframe is complete, it's hard work. It requires a lot of perseverance: the persistence to keep doing things that we feel are going against the grain. But then, at some point, it simply clicks, and we find we have automated this new practice within our brains.

It goes without saying that certain changes take fewer days and less effort, while others demand more. The number cited by Clear is an average. It highlights the need to understand that change takes time and persistence. But what's important to note here is that focusing on that number in order to see if the concept works may be a mere defense mechanism for dismissing an argument regardless of its validity. Our intellect justifies our actions and creates a story that rejects new possibilities. That is to say that many of the big changes we seek to make – within ourselves, our teams, or our organizations – won't happen until we change the way we change. To do this, we must first change the way we look at the world and interpret the stories we use to give meaning to what happens, creating new stories to help us become more effective and enjoy the journey more. We are challenged to look at what is happening around us and to consider what we can and cannot do using new mindsets that make us more efficient by helping us first understand what is holding us back.

# **5.** The enemies of change

When we decide to change something, to learn and improve, and we commit to that better version of ourselves, a series of subconscious mechanisms unfold that are difficult to perceive. They are happening, but silently, in the background. Our ability to achieve what we want depends on our ability to acknowledge and think through these mechanisms, rather than simply declaring our intent. Over the next few pages, we will look at the most relevant inhibitors. We will shine a spotlight on them in order to begin to rethink them and, little by little, break them down in our first step toward a new way of changing.

The most significant limiting factors – and ones which largely depend on us – are:

our **brains** trying to preserve energy;

our **egos**, our self-perception and quest for perfection;

sacrificing **form** in the quest for quick results; and

wanting something without being prepared to pay the **price**.

Now, let's delve into the specifics of each of these "enemies," so that we can turn them into allies that can help us take the next step forward.

## Brain economy

Every day, we do hundreds of things on autopilot. We don't even question them. We don't wonder if we have to do them or not – we simply do them. We reproduce these behaviors as if they had a mind of their own.

If we tried to count how many decisions like these we make each day, we would probably lose count. Very few decisions are conscious. It would be like having to think about every step we take when walking; life would become impossible. It would be neither efficient nor feasible.

However, we often lack the necessary habits to overcome the new challenges we encounter. In other words, we simply don't have the habits that would most help us to achieve what we want and to set our intentions in motion.

In a disruptive world that never stops, the biggest differentiating factor will lie in learning to adapt and become more agile at developing new habits that help us to re-think ourselves. If we can do this, progressing and transforming won't be an effort, but an enjoyable new habit that will motivate and galvanize us. This will help us to adapt in the face of new circumstances and choose how we accomplish meaningful progress and change.

Sometimes, the status quo makes it difficult to think with an open mind and different perspective. As we grow and integrate a variety of ecosystems, restrictions begin to appear. Our behavior conforms to the incentives and obstacles that each individual system defines as correct or incorrect, and we in turn become conditioned to create automatic responses in accordance with each of these systems.

Later, we will look in more detail at the main systems to which we belong.

Changing, evolving and transforming shouldn't be a constant effort. It can also be a new habit that energizes us. It all depends on our outlook.

Our central nervous system has a lot of responses. As our interests, desires and needs change, so do our systems. This means that, at some point, the habits we rely on can no longer resolve new challenges – but we keep turning to them regardless. It's actually difficult for us to question them. But why? Because that's what we learned. Because our minds respond to stimuli. Because it's what we think we are supposed to do. Because we are often afraid to do it any other way. Because sometimes, we don't even realize we are doing it. Because, although we would rationally prefer to do things a different way (a way that would make us more efficient, and perhaps happier), we find it hard to get out of the inertia. It is difficult to step back, breathe for a minute, focus our minds and turn off that autopilot.

## The ego and the lack of logic

Much of what I learned in those first few years coincided with one of the sharpest – and most counterintuitive – ideas that Nithya shared with me during one of our many chats:

> Wisdom? Wisdom is not believing our own thoughts.

I think most people will know what I mean. But, in general, we do the opposite. We believe everything we think. We believe we can see reality. We judge everything and everyone, and we keep doing it, never stopping to look at what is truly important to us. What we want to accomplish. What connects with our values. And this is not just because of our automatic habits: it's our vanity, ego, constant judgement of ourselves – and its flipside and best ally, perfectionism – that make it so difficult for us to listen to ourselves and to others.

Many of our obsessions reside in that disconnect: our repetitive behaviors, our defensiveness over our image, our desire for short-term results and exclusively positive emotions.

If we pay attention, it's amazing just how unaware we are of these near-invisible social addictions. I often hear people complaining about the younger generation (because everyone looks back with rose-tinted glasses), but how many of us, with more years under our belts and more life experience, still seek immediate answers and constant recognition?

Just think about how different the energy is in places where mirrors show us our own image reflected back: in an elevator, in an activity at the gym, in the bathroom, on our cellphones, on the computer screen, in the photos and quotes we post on social media, on chat messages, videocalls and virtual meetings on Zoom, Teams or whatever platform we use. It becomes irresistible to look at that reflected image – sometimes, to reaffirm how satisfied we are with ourselves, and sometimes to criticize ourselves mercilessly, but always to measure and judge ourselves. We love to look at ourselves. Looking at our reflection in a mirror, watching what we are doing, looking at what we believe we need, looking at what we believe other people need, without really asking them.

We feel that that makes us who we are. In the same way, we believe that if we do not fulfil our own expectations, our whole world could fall apart. We distract ourselves with our own stories, and that stops us from connecting with others as well as with our own deepest desires.

All of this atrophies the muscles of our flexibility and hinders our ability to evolve freely, to look at every situation and at the future as an opportunity rather than as uncertain terrain.

It's tempting to invest energy into looking at our own image, rather than looking for what's behind it. But if we focus on ourselves, then what happens when we have to acknowledge, deep down, that we don't know something, that something is difficult, that someone else can do something better and faster, or that we need time and effort to learn something? That image we project is thrown into crisis. The mirror shatters.

Without really understanding how or why, we lay our heads on our pillows, remember a situation from that day, and think: "Why did I say that?" And how are we supposed to tell other people that we need help or that we made a mistake when we believe that our own image is in jeopardy?

## The most dangerous bias: we all think we're the best

There have been several studies about people's self-assessment when asked how good they are at driving. Almost everyone gives the same result. I use this when I deliver conferences and work with teams. Generally speaking, I ask those present how they see their organization, their teams, and – finally – their own ability to implement change aimed at achieving better results (this could be a novelty everyone is trying to take on, a different mindset, new behaviors that the organization's leaders have declared is key for strategy, and so on). Then, I ask them to assign a points value to each group (their organization, the team present in the room, and the individual members themselves) from 1 (*does nothing*) to 10 (*does it perfectly*). Most answers follow the same trend:

a rating of between 4 and 5 for the organization;

between 5 and 7 for the team;

between 7 and 9 for themselves.

Yes, this is mathematically impossible: if each individual is better than the average, and rates themselves between 7 and 9 points, how can the average for each group – and the organization itself – be lower than that?

Something doesn't add up. But these are the results that come back time and time again. What is going wrong? It's our great cognitive bias: we think we are better than the rest.

## Careful: pride comes before a fall

Have you ever wondered why inspirational talks with new methodologies always have an impact at the time, but don't bear out their effectiveness over time? It's because, subconsciously, almost everyone present draws the same conclusion from their own bias: "This is basic! Other people need to start doing it," or "I got it, I already know how to do this." Sound familiar?

Now, I want to suggest a very simple exercise. Call to mind a person who you consider could really benefit from this book and its ideas (an invitation to change and improve). Do you have that person's name in mind? Now, imagine this situation: that person has this book in their hands, and, when I ask them the same question, they think of your name.

## We want to come across as perfect

Anyone who learns from their vulnerability will be able to resolve their problems much faster – possibly even enjoying them – than someone who hides behind an ego built around perfection. However, this is totally counterintuitive in the society in which we were raised and of which we are now a part.

We inherited a world in which we learned to obtain recognition when we display knowledge, confidence and certainty, and where we have to achieve "good grades" in order to gain approval. Our brains learn that when we are young. Then, in adulthood, that experience hinders our ability to experiment, to say "I don't know," to make mistakes, to learn new things and to change fast. In short, it keeps us from bringing our best version to life in any situation. After all, when we don't know something, is it better to hide it? Or is it better to say it out loud, so that we can quickly learn what it is our team needs from us?

Brené Brown, a researcher at the University of Houston, has been working for some time on the relevance of vulnerability to leadership in the modern world. Her research debunks the myth that perfection is the most effective way. The titles of some of her books say it all: *The Gifts of Imperfection* (2010), *The Power of Vulnerability* (2012), and her latest book, *Dare to Lead* (2019). I recommend reading these books as a first cognitive step to understanding what this practice is all about, why we find it so hard to connect with the part of ourselves that can transform and inspire others, and how to begin doing so.

The most interesting balance Brown attempts to achieve when writing and talking about her experiences in various online talks is that of telling personal stories with vulnerability and without trying to come across as perfect. Look for that balance between being inspirational in your own challenges ("I did it, you can do it too") and the idea of constant progress ("And this is a never-ending journey that I will have to keep trying at"). I think that's why she connects with people so well. She hits a nerve and makes people want to do things that their protective brains are trying to avoid doing.

We all lose our balance, we fall, we fail, we feel pain. That's because we all face situations that hurt, that affect us, that present new challenges. We are not machines. But sometimes, we don't like to show it – and when we hide that part of ourselves, we live as if we could disconnect some areas of ourselves from others, as if we were a set of pieces rather than a living organism, internally interconnected and linked to our entire ecosystem.

In organizations, many people avoid talking about their emotions, since it is associated with appearing vulnerable and fragile in others' eyes. This idea of a world where leadership is associated with masculine energy and where leaders must be strong and unbreakable is fortunately being questioned and reconsidered. We have learned that that no longer works, that it is not always that way, and that it doesn't connect with people looking for

Vulnerability is not winning or losing; it's having the courage to show up and be seen when we have no control over the outcome. Vulnerability is not weakness; it's our greatest measure of courage.

BRENÉ BROWN

reasons to commit and give it their all. Changing this paradigm and acting accordingly is part of our own personal challenge, too.

When we talk about things that affect or condition us, expressing who we are in the most conducive and effective way depending on the context brings our emotions to the forefront when it comes to making decisions, understanding what affects and worries us, and – above all – what we want, both collectively and as individuals.

## The way we do things, matters

The rate of change is very intense in our modern society. What's more, our attachment to what we know is deep-seated. That's why, when we protect our own situations, we feel exposed to the unknown and to that which we cannot control. By following our egos, we act according to what authority figures will think – our parents when we were children, our bosses now that we're adults, someone *successful* when we feel under pressure – instead of acting according to our own values or our own standards of success and happiness.

We all agree that it is important to obtain tangible results. What we sometimes forget is that, in order for this to happen, we must not sacrifice the process in all its forms. In the long run, those momentary results are seen for what they are: a mirage. Our purpose and our intentions are what will prevail.

In order to assess our intentions and purpose, we can ask ourselves some questions which – if answered honestly – can help guide us toward new discoveries.

In my case, given my own intentions (which I shared with you on page 41), the most important questions would be:

Emotions are never a threat. They are a great source of information for understanding what is happening to us, gaining awareness, and becoming more effective.

Have I connected with people and the situation while being 100% present?

Was I helpful to other people?

Did I challenge them kindly, to be the best possible versions of themselves?

And finally, to turn the experience itself into an opportunity:

What did I learn?

What am I proud of, given how I acted?

What would I try doing differently?

## What questions would we ask ourselves?

### When results are the only driving factor

In terms of results, success will always depend on many factors outside our control. On the other hand, the success of our process will never depend on external factors: we will always be the axis. Focusing exclusively on immediate results hides the fact that, during the process, we can also achieve other valuable aims: we can build trust, honor our own beliefs, strengthen our team, and be more noble and conscientious leaders. We can act in accordance with our intentions.

A common belief for justifying past habits is that people who are good during the process and who have values do not necessarily obtain positive results. Another prevalent misconception is that the only way to get results is to sacrifice our values. In reality, a person who values the accomplishment of certain aims will integrate results into the process itself. Learning from every situation is of fundamental value to becoming more effective. The big difference is that this places the focus on learning from every situation, rather than merely admiring our achievements (and egos) when we reach goals, and punishing ourselves when we don't.

Some spiritual practices talk about "dissolving the ego," though I don't actually suggest going as far as that. The question I invite you to ask yourself is: How can you build an ego that rests on your values and your most virtuous behaviors? I simply invite you to reflect on how you can construct an ego that rejoices in what you consider conducive to your well-being, happiness, and purpose, acting in a way that is aligned with your values, and – when that's not possible – prioritizing your values over results.

## Being prepared to "pay the price"

Whenever we want to obtain something, we are ready to pay a price. We do it every day, with every decision we make, every product we buy, and every service we hire someone for. We know – or, at least, we think – that the benefit will correspond with the price we paid. We know that some effort is required now in order to obtain a future benefit, more or less immediate.

In every learning process, acknowledging what we don't know and allowing ourselves to be vulnerable in the eyes of others – and our own – is not just a way of dissolving our egos: it is the price we must pay in order to get closer to doing things the way we should be doing them. The key to progress lies less in our current ability to tackle that task, and more in what we consider to be the main factor in change and whether we dare to lay bare our own current lack of ability.

We all have more to learn. All of us. But it's not about just learning something – it's about daring to "raise our hands" and recognize that we need to keep learning, without feeling exposed or fragile as a result.

# 6. Not everything is the same: the different types of change

## Adaptation, evolution, and transformation

Rationally, we know that we could do things differently, and in many situations, we would like to. However, we find it difficult to set the necessary changes in motion, even though we know that the things that make us feel fulfilled and satisfied are the sum of all those little actions: every conversation we hold, every time we connect with an emotion or genuinely listen to the person we are speaking to, every time we begin a project that inspires us, every time we make a decision that takes someone else into account. Depending on our intentions, we can establish the extent to which we are aligned with them.

So, why does this dissociation happen? One of the main causes is the subconscious belief that all change shares the same nature. It may be that we never stop to think about this dynamic and try to distinguish between the different changes in each situation. We are not fully aware that there are various levels of complexity at play.

It's true that there are many things we can understand, implement or resolve in a relatively short space of time. We are able to change and improve, or simply to adapt to new situations. There are numerous examples: from traveling to a new country and quickly adjusting to the time zone, to going from living alone to living with friends or a partner.

We are used to constantly changing and adapting, but those are not the kinds of changes we are talking about when we want to make a qualitative leap or get ready for a significant new challenge. It's about another kind of change: The kind we declared we intended to make years ago, the kind our companies require from us in the face of new obstacles, or the kind that will better connect us with our own happiness, getting us closer to our dreams and aspirations. The problem is that these changes often remain exactly that: dreams. They stay as desires and aspirations that eventually turn into frustrations, ultimately reinforcing our perception that change is difficult.

But the real question is not about the specific change concerned or its circumstantial context – it's about how we can make the process of change possible. In other words: How can we change the way we change? When we modify that, we will ourselves change, and with that, change the world around us. To do this, we must begin by understanding the nature of the changes we want to make.

To begin with, we will differentiate between four types of change, each of which requires a different type of response.

I am going to use sporting metaphors to explain them. The tension that we feel when making these changes is somewhat similar to the physical exertion involved in practicing various types of sports.

The wisdom to understand that different challenges need different solutions is the first step to being effective. There are four different types of change.

**1)** Just exercising

**2)** Training to play a sport (socially)

**3)** Running a marathon

**4)** Getting into a new sport

## **1)** Exercising

EFFORT: **LOW**

There are certain changes that most people can make with relative ease. One example could be making the decision to do a little workout a couple of days each week. We know that it is beneficial and that we can do it if we set our minds to it, whether it's tagging along with a friend to the gym or going for a walk to get our heart rates up a little. It's enough to recognize that we want to do something a different way and simply start doing it. Nothing about it goes against our values, beliefs or customs. It is relatively easy to incorporate into our current lifestyle.

This category also includes all the changes we make daily without even realizing. They arise from our ability to adapt to our circumstances. Examples include incorporating a new food that we enjoy into our diet on a doctor's advice, leaving our car keys in a designated tray so that we can find them more easily, going to a new store for groceries, or simply doing something easy our boss asks us to do. In short, everything we integrate into our lives without really noticing. However, when we shine a light on these changes and begin to acknowledge and appreciate the fact that we made them, they become a great resource for our brains to get ready for the more relevant challenges still to come.

## 2) Training  EFFORT: **MODERATE**

There are some more demanding changes that require the incorporation of certain skills and more consistent practice than before. Sometimes, they even require us to lay ourselves bare, allowing ourselves to be vulnerable and asking others for feedback to help us progress. The sports-related example here would be going from getting some exercise to being a part of a team, or practicing a sport that requires a minimum level of fitness. This means we have to train more often – perhaps even alongside others, who may play a casual role in helping us to move forward.

Translated into everyday situations, this happens when, for example, we decide to completely remove from our diets something we've been consuming habitually for years (ever tried to go cold turkey on sugar?), or commit to separating our recycling trash, or are asked by our bosses to upload information to a new system and we don't know how to use it. In many of these cases, in a couple of days, weeks, or months, we can improve and incorporate those changes permanently, in such a way that they become the new status quo. They become second nature, part of our routine. Of course, these processes require energy, because we have to learn something new rather than simply exercising what we already knew, but we can do it by ourselves. We modify a few behaviors, practice a little, and feel the challenge becoming more feasible as the days go on. Not only do we understand it, but for various reasons, we don't find it so difficult to get started and turn it into part of our routine. Our own willpower and the knowledge we can acquire by ourselves are enough to train us to rise to the challenge. There are several changes we make that are like this.

## 3) Running a marathon

EFFORT: **SUSTAINED**

While I'm only an amateur runner, I have completed two marathons so far. The vast majority of people I know, whether they know it or not, are (or could be) fit enough to run a marathon. I don't know if they would say the same, but I would bet on their ability to do it. Of course, that isn't enough.

There are two things stopping it from happening: stories constructed about the effort it takes to make a big change, and the difficulty of sustaining discipline for the amount of time it takes to reach a better version of ourselves. At the beginning of these processes of change, just like in a marathon, we need someone to share their experiences with us, to guide us and keep us going through the tough moments (and those will come, sooner or later). Whether we call them a coach, leader, trainer, experienced friend, or whatever else, beyond their title or label, the idea is always the same: some changes require more than what we are currently capable of achieving yet. It's as simple as that: we need support.

No one prepares for a marathon in their bedroom, alone, eating the same way they always did, reading books and watching shows on how to run. You need the right diet, a good "trainer," and a solid internal commitment to not giving up on the first rainy day or with the first pulled muscle. And this is just the preparation: the marathon itself comes much later. Training to change the way our muscles burn energy, adapting to new foods, increasing our aerobic capacity, strengthening our minds to enjoy long training sessions and races – all of this takes around sixteen weeks.

The process is clear and accessible for anyone to understand. But to run and enjoy running, you have to do it, not just understand it. These experiences make us appreciate the value of determination and action. That's why we sometimes need someone else: someone to check up on us to make sure we're staying on track, or someone to go out running with come rain or shine, because their role is to help us remember what we said was

The most important thing is to remember the most important thing.

SUZUKI ROSHI

important to us. They help us not to fall at the first hurdle – and that hurdle will crop up sooner or later.

The satisfaction this leads to is boundless. So much so that we tend to want to do it all again. Because we can connect with the pleasure of having put in the effort, of having been able to change a deep-seated belief and of having undergone a transformation that takes us to a place from which we can no longer see the world the way we did before.

## Asking, accepting and acting

Here is one of the factors that makes it so difficult to effect meaningful change: we don't like asking for help. And it's not just that: we also don't like accepting it. But, above all, we don't like putting ourselves in the hands of someone who knows more than us about a given topic that we believe we should be naturally good at.

When I ran my first marathon, I thought the key was simply to run and run. Nothing could be further from the truth. Without help, I don't think I would have been able to do it. There are some things that we can't do if we don't challenge our own beliefs and practices. It's as simple as that. We are not born athletes, nor are we born to be the best leaders, parents, or friends. We are not automatically prepared for everything we want to do with our futures.

In a process of transformation, a large portion of our success lies in agreeing to other people becoming "guardians" of our process, which means we have to defer to their knowledge without letting our egos get in the way. Above all, we have to learn the humility to accept our limitations and keep on practicing. This gives our guide the chance to challenge us without being questioned.

Remember: if we knew how to do it on our own, we would be doing it already.

Life is the journey
we go on to expand
our abilities.

## Connecting with our own example

Before looking at the fourth type of change, let's do an exercise. Think about your own story, in real and specific episodes. Think about a situation where you were able to genuinely make a change that was important to you and for which you had to give up some deep-seated habits.

You can use questions such as the following as a guide:

---

What kind of change was it?

---

How much effort did it require?

---

What did you have to do to achieve it?

---

Who supported you and how?

---

Whenever I talk about topics like this in public, just like I am doing now in this book, I get the sensation I am not saying anything new. I even question the value of asking these questions. That's when I realize the need to make this clarification: the value of reflecting on these topics lies not in their novelty (since they are nothing new), but rather in profoundly understanding the implications of truly changing something, moving to the next level, and expanding our abilities.

We all have experiences where we were able to transform something and others where, on the contrary, we could not. If we look back, with both an empathetic and a critical eye, we find so many experiences that can help us if we just find a way to connect with them.

Just by going back over the conversations we hold every day with friends, relatives and colleagues, we find all kinds of stories. How many times have you heard (or said!): "Diet starts tomorrow"? How many diets really do start the next day? How many last long enough to generate new habits? How many are abandoned with some excuse before reaching the necessary turning point? If we know that going out for a walk, run or bike ride a couple of times a week is healthy, why do we put it off week after week? Most of us say we want to do things, but we only try them occasionally – and even when we try them, we struggle to maintain them over time.

So, if it's so hard to make any changes that require a moderate to considerable level of effort, why do we expect it to be any easier to make changes requiring the transformation of our most deeply rooted habits and beliefs? We tend to believe that all change requires more or less the same effort: that simply by *wanting* to do something, we will be able to.

We want to believe that all change – even the most aspirational, demanding kind – involves moderate, quick effort that doesn't cost us too much. All you have to do is run a little more. Start Monday, and then everything will just fall into place. It's that simple, that far from reality, that common.

But wishing alone won't get us to our goals. Not everyone experiences the same problems. We know, deep down, when we are trying to run a marathon unprepared. That's why one of the fundamental elements of every learning or changing process is to have a "guardian" whom we authorize to call us out on the things our *enemies of change* are trying to protect.

## 4) Playing a new sport — EFFORT: **UNKNOWN**

There are so many sports we are unfamiliar with, with rules, moves, guidelines and techniques we have never attempted. When adults try something for the first time without having done it as children, when they had the capacity to absorb and learn things subconsciously, the challenge is enormous. It's not just about how difficult it is to do – it's about how much more difficult it is to accept that we don't know how to do something.

The world is changing so fast. New knowledge, technology, theories and methodologies are constantly being developed. If we want to be a part of it, we cannot keep believing that what we learned ten, twenty or thirty years ago is still valid today. We know that, but it's still difficult to accept the idea of once again having to study in order to learn new things. Paradoxically, though it is when we are adults that we most need to develop new tools to stay in touch with the world around us, that is when we dedicate the least energy to doing so. Why? Perhaps it's because all those mental blocks we have are activated simultaneously. Who's going to teach me something, with my big professional career, with hundreds of people under me and all the big business deals I close? Why would I go back to formal studies, when I'm a parent and it's my kids who go to school now? Why would I need lessons when I'm a successful adult with the respect of my colleagues? Our minds ask themselves questions like these, even if we don't realize it. The problem, in this case, is not the questions themselves but the answers we have for them. When we realize what these profound changes involve, every warning light on the *enemies of change* board starts flashing at once: ego, vulnerability, perfectionism, *what will people say*, judgments we think others will make, and above all, our own judgments and our own minds, who constantly whisper in our ears all the things that hold us back from doing what we want. And we go through life this way: explaining to everyone how important it is to learn, progress, transform, and change, while debating with ourselves on how to do that without having to expose ourselves. How to get results without taking any risks. How to maintain our image based on knowledge, rather than creating one based on what we have yet to learn in order to keep growing.

If we don't break this cycle, we will become expert know-it-alls, telling everyone else what they need to do to improve without ever putting it into practice ourselves.

### Start studying again (and never stop!)

Recognizing that there are different types of change requires a greater degree of awareness of our own limitations: it means being able to say: "I don't know how to do it yet, I'm going to need some help." Appealing to that vulnerability is a source of energy for beginning the journey that enables us to be good learners. That same vulnerability requires admitting that perhaps we are not as perfect as we believe, or seem, or would like to be.

There is a traditional path of progress that we all know and many of us have been lucky enough to follow: attending school up to a certain age, possibly college until we were twenty-something, then a professional career, perhaps a master's, then work, work, work, learning everything we can while working, starting a family, and just watching life go by. Any resemblance to actual life is not purely coincidental.

## Living in a world that no longer exists

Life has changed so much in comparison with the norm of thirty or forty years ago, when we learned one profession and stayed in that job until we retired. Today, almost all of us have to reinvent ourselves within our jobs, or move from one profession to another. In candidate selection processes, it's becoming less and less important what a person studied, and more important to know that they can reinvent themselves and use the knowledge they have to adapt to an ever-changing world. That is why we have to learn, acquire new skills, and be flexible, regardless of our age or background.

There are endless new things to learn. The problem lies in choosing the things that correspond to our intentions. Today, we have the very real opportunity to study many disciplines and connect with many different worlds, but nevertheless we rarely consider learning in this way. It's nearly always about just "doing a course," rather than entering that never-ending cycle of constant development, using everything at our disposal to continue growing.

The Covid-19 pandemic gave us – and is still giving us – the chance to dive into new fields far removed from our everyday jobs, or to reinforce ideas and methods from a fresh perspective. Once again, opportunity arises from crises. In this new world, in which we are barely ever asked to have a formal qualification, let us learn and incorporate new ways of thinking about things and of doing things so that we are always well prepared. Let us integrate new knowledge not for its inherent value but for the "mental elasticity" it affords us.

We have the great opportunity to reconnect with our experimental mode.

## Ready for the challenges of tomorrow

I often use a question posed by economist and technologist Santiago Bilinkis to the audience at *Coloquio Idea*, one of the biggest gatherings of leading executives in Argentina. "Who here wants their children to learn computer programming at school?" he asked. Almost all hands went up. Then, another question, which wiped the smiles off the audience's faces: "And who among you know how to program or intend to study it?" Only one or two hands went up. A third question took them from thin smiles to trying to think of an example: "Why should your children do it, but not you? Why, when you still have twenty or thirty years left of adding value in the world of work and your lives in general, do you think that it's only important for your kids and not for yourselves?"

It's not about knowing programming, or learning a new language. It's about daring to incorporate a new type of logic: how to think outside the box to solve problems, how to think about the modern world, how to be a part of things with no prejudice and no fear of what people will say, how to reach something as yet unknown. That's why the "back-to-school" that I suggest here is not necessarily about studying for a new career or acquiring any specific knowledge. What I suggest is learning new ways of thinking and of doing things, to keep on preparing ourselves for the life we still have ahead of us.

Never stopping studying is a way to keep ourselves curious and turn ourselves into perpetual "learners," where every conversation, action and exchange becomes an experience that teaches us something new. To stay in shape, to take care of our minds, to make them a little more flexible every day. To stay agile, and to enjoy the journey.

## I'll pay you to study!

Generally speaking, the organizations to which we belong not only understand this, but actually consider it fundamental for the future. However, not many of them create enough genuine opportunities for people to learn how to learn, or to improve their mental flexibility. Every company wants to be more innovative, more agile, more appealing to the best talent – so why not innovate in the way they create these opportunities?

So far, I don't see many companies backing a new standard: for example, their employees could dedicate ten or twenty per cent of their working time to learning something new – something they like and which motivates them – purely so that they become better at absorbing skills with curiosity and flexibility. I don't mean those typical "study days" given to those doing formal courses, nor do I mean time given only to those who have recently joined the company – in fact, the people who have been there years are the ones who need it most – but rather, offering an integrated program. This could involve a four-day working week, with the fifth day devoted to development, growth and learning, for example. Or one week every quarter where each person does a course with the main aim of broadening their horizons. If we want to create agile, flexible and innovative people, why don't we give that a try?

I write this in the hope that some companies will go above and beyond and improve upon this idea. Others may try to put it into practice, and others still may offer five per cent of the time, once a month, with the condition that it must be something of use to the company and requiring a monthly presentation by the employee. As if the only things that have value are those presented in PowerPoint presentations.

Whatever you think when you read about this idea speaks to your mindset, your beliefs, and how open you are to experimenting, seeing what happens, and learning from personal experience. Don't let this be one more example of trying to implement good ideas with the best of intentions but ending up killing them off by doing them with the same old mindset.

So, for those of you interested in trying something different and seeing what happens, I invite you to try it with just one condition: get into "learning mode" right away. Don't spend weeks agonizing and analyzing what to do, paralyzed in your quest for the perfect idea. I invite you to make yourself a part of the change experiment, by looking for evidence within actions themselves.

three

# We are not alone:

## The impact of the ecosystems to which we belong

In this proud land we grew up strong
We were wanted all along
I was taught to fight, taught to win, I never thought I could fail ... Don't give up, 'cause you have friends ... Don't give up, I know you can make it good

PETER GABRIEL, "*Don't Give up.*"

**https://spoti.fi/3kOvFEQ**

If you want to listen to the song from the original Spanish version of the book, check it out here

https://spoti.fi/3fUFz4G

For over fifteen years now, ninety per cent of communication in my job has been in English. I don't speak it perfectly, but I can get by. I can work all over the world without language posing an issue, and that's something I'm very proud of. I studied English between the ages of six and eighteen, and then I gave it up almost completely until I was twenty-three. At one point, I needed to work with people from various places around the world, and English was a fundamental communication tool. In my case, I could understand and read relatively well, but I still needed a lot of practice, especially when it came to writing. That's why I made a decision that seemed risky, and which I admit I was unsure about. I sent an email to every native English speaker I worked with to ask them to spend five minutes, every time I had a conversation with them or sent them an email, giving me a little feedback and correcting my English. I even began some meetings by saying: "Please correct me if I make mistakes when speaking." It wasn't easy. I had a bad time with it on occasion – not just because of my clumsy English, but because of the avalanche of corrections I began to receive.

At first, I felt a little bothered – irritated, even. Remember that I had asked for this. People were constantly correcting me in the middle of conversations, whether via chat (MSN, in those days!) or email. I received dozens of emails every day where people pointed out where I had spelled things wrong, and I even got interrupted in the middle of arguments.

It was only after a while that I was able to feel grateful for that experiment.

That happened when I began to notice my progress, when I got used to this new habit, when I realized that I was getting better, meeting by meeting, and also that many people were enjoying helping me out. It was as if I was taking something other people could already see and putting it on the table to make it part of the conversation. Somehow, it stopped being taboo. That was when I really started to improve exponentially, and I felt much more confident at doing my job in English now that I had the ability to go with the flow of important conversations without worrying about whether or not people could understand me – and I could understand others better, too.

# 7. A little bit of culture

When we started Axialent in 2003, we focused on creating an organization with an impact on the leaders of large institutions and companies. We wanted to be able to change the way they thought and acted; we wanted to change that world with the significant impact it has on society, raise awareness of who we were, establish new ways of doing things, and think about how the skills of all those leaders could be developed in order to do them. We always thought that leaders projected their own shadow over an organization, and the quality of that shadow has a significant impact on decisions made regarding how to reach goals and how to create space for people to develop.

Fred Kofman's book *Conscious Business* perfectly expressed all those ideas and practices that aimed to renew and consolidate Fred's work in his previous trilogy, *Metamanagement*. Four years of rapid growth, impact and expansion had gone into it. Fred's brilliant work – not only in putting those ideas on paper, but in being part of a system that trained consultants who could take those suggestions to companies all over the world – was the open secret to those early years of success.

The problem came when we realized that this strategy had its limits. We began to notice that despite our training people in masse and carrying out other profound interventions in the highest levels of these organizations, the impact over time wasn't quite as effective as we had hoped. We were planting many seeds, but only a few were sprouting. We also realized that many of the participants in these training courses did, in fact, apply the new concepts they had learned to other areas of their lives (for example, with their families), but that it required too much effort to do so for their companies, so the changes they were aiming for never quite materialized.

## Resistance

So, what obstacles did we manage to identify? Systems of belonging, deep-seated values, beliefs, habits: all those structures proved stronger than any new ideas, than the desire for change and for new practices. These people wanted to change, and they tried to – they just couldn't.

That's when Carolyn Taylor and her team came on board. Carolyn signed up with all of her characteristic energy, all her experience, and a great team of people. Through the use of many of her methods and with the members of her team (among them Cathy Glass, a great colleague with whom I worked for many more years afterward), we managed to find the missing piece and zero in on something that almost no one was talking about back in 2006: organizational culture. From that moment on, we resolved to learn and develop new practices and skills that would enable us to link *leadership* with *culture*, like two sides of the same coin.

For me, it was a fresh stroke of luck. During my first few years at Axialent, I worked shoulder-to-shoulder with Fred – not just on the team developing the consultancy manual and internal training processes, but also on events aimed at selecting and developing consultants around the world (although I learned most from conversations with him and the team during dinners or hikes, whether in Boulder, Singapore or Buenos Aires). Now, I also had the chance to work shoulder-to-shoulder with Carolyn, learning how to design proposals, work with clients and have those deep talks at the end of an intense working day somewhere in the world, when learning is off the charts.

As a side gig, I oversaw the translation of her book into Spanish, and so the book "*La cultura del ejemplo*" (Literal translation would be The Culture of being an example, but the original version was named Walking the talk) was born. I learned so much, not even realizing that I was getting ready to lead the European region at Axialent, and Carolyn worked alongside me there for the first year. She had the great gift of making me, and all of us who worked with her, feel important, valued and autonomous. That was another great lesson in leadership that has stayed with me ever since.

This launched Axialent into the world of organizational culture, to the point that we became a benchmark for helping leaders and organizations to connect their actions and decisions with the systemic impact they have, and vice versa. This background on how I got into this field is the best way I can explain why, if we want to change, improve and create transformations to connect with the best versions of ourselves, it's not enough to look in our individual mirrors. We also need to look at the context and ecosystems to which we belong.

## One and the universe

We are part of systems that condition us, incentivize us, inhibit us. This creates stories, customs and habits: in other words, various belief systems. Almost without questioning it, we think, feel and act in a context predetermined by certain factors.

Look, for example, at how we behave in a football stadium compared to how we behave at a dinner party with a colleague or boss and their family. Similarly, think about how we greet our friends versus how we greet people we have just met. Or how we feel getting around a city we just arrived in, or how we drive in a country we've never been to before. Systems and cultures create guidelines and benchmarks that provide order and lend meaning to our ideas and behaviors. They also help us save time, since we don't have to constantly think about what to do and say.

To change aspects of ourselves and behave in ways more closely aligned with our purpose and intentions, we first must understand the cultures of the ecosystems to which we belong. When we make the invisible visible, we can choose how to rise to the challenge: by modifying the culture (if possible), by contending with some of its inconsistencies, or by abandoning it (if we don't feel that it is helping us). But this last option is not so easy. Why not? Because we tend to identify with the systems we belong to, so questioning or abandoning them requires a vast amount of effort. But there is no greater freedom than the opportunity to choose. To stay where we are and with the people we are with because we want to, not because it's less effort. All of this means that becoming aware of that which we were previously unaware of is a great way to exercise our freedom.

## Making the invisible visible

While culture – at least, in the sense that we are viewing it in this chapter – is present everywhere, at all times, we don't always see it. It is intangible. That's why making the invisible visible is the first step to changing, modifying or improving a culture. It means becoming aware of what is going on: of things we may have sensed but probably could not yet see clearly. To help with this task, I present to you an analysis of three systems to which we all belong in the modern world: the society we grew up in, the cities where we live, and the organizations we belong to.

# 8. The society we grow up in

We will refer to society, in shorthand, to give context and help understand how the sources of cultural creation function. Then, we will go a little beyond that and look at how the place where we grow up and live can change the way we interact with the world much more profoundly than we believed. And finally, we will delve into the world of organizations in detail, to look at how organizational culture works and to connect with some of the situations we experience on a daily basis.

## How can it be that my children...?

Every time I give a talk centered around the concept of culture, I use a book that I find simple and entertaining: Tim Parks' 1995 book *An Italian Education*. This book follows the children of an Englishman who has been living in Italy for ten years with his Italian wife, and how the children, little by little, *become* Italian.

It's an ingenious and somewhat cynical look at an expat's attempts to raise his children in a society different from his own. In a country with one of the lowest birth rates in the world (1.4 per family at that time), he believes that

Italian children are spoiled and pampered from the day they are born. For an English atheist like himself, it's excessive. But it's not just the children who receive an 'Italian education'; he himself learns to be a parent there, with all the changes that involves for his English history. Parks narrates his adventures with the local legal system, which, in true Anglo-Saxon fashion, often proves absurd and contradictory.

How do his children learn to be the way they are? What, if any, English traditions still influence them? How does one become a paid-up member of society in their country of birth? How can an expat fit into a new society? What are the children of expats? Where do they belong? I use these questions to encapsulate how a culture is created, before applying it to other systems which we navigate every day in order to study the forces that contain and impact us in every single thing we do, say and think.

Firstly, I will list some of the most relevant sources of cultural creation:

---

The education system: what values, practices and objectives it is based on;

---

What our peers do: how our friends and classmates play, learn and live;

---

What our mentors do: adults, in particular our parents, our parents' friends, our grandparents and our teachers;

---

The media: film, television, radio, newspapers and – in recent years – social media;

---

Religion and the legal system: the predominant values and belief systems that influence our ethics and create reward and punishment, whether real or imaginary;

---

Language, with words that actually exist (or not) and which we can therefore use, the words we invent through dialects (Southern, inner-city, Northwest, and so on) or slang;

Symbols: stories and legends told to us and which we then retell.

If we can sustainably change systems, symbols and the behaviors of key leaders, we will be able to change what people believe is expected of them. That is how we change culture.

Later, we will look at how this applies to the organizations to which we belong or with which we interact, and what direct implications it has. Now, let's look at how societies are formed, how they might be reconsidered, and how their cultures can be modified.

## The Swedish Theory of Love

In 2015, Italian director Erik Gandini debuted his haunting movie The Swedish Theory of Love (*La teoria svedese dell'amore*). The film explores how a country many hold up as a model, thanks to its progress in recent decades, is actually experiencing extensive social problems.

In 1972, the Swedish government under Sven Olof Palme published a manifesto entitled "The Family of the Future: A Socialist Family Policy." It aimed to lay the groundwork for a State policy revolving around the concept of the family, and it maintained that "every genuine human relationship must be supported by the principle of independence between people." This is a clear declaration of purpose, values and intentions. Around four decades later, the policy was confirmed to be successful...if we focus on its great intentions. The problem is that the world has changed, and so have people, and this shared wish of the Swedes – for which they created a belief system that worked – generated unwanted side effects. The exaltation of individual self-sufficiency meant that one in every two Swedes lived most of their lives alone, and one in four died the same way.

As the director explained at the time of the movie's release, "All genuine human relationships must be based on fundamental independence between people. If a woman depends on a man, how do we know she is voluntarily in that relationship? Children have many rights. Elderly people no longer rely on the goodwill of their adult children. The ideal family in Sweden is made up of adult individuals who are fundamentally independent. Independent and working for themselves."

*The Swedish Theory of Love* demonstrated that loneliness had become a serious side effect of the policy, and it actually went against its original spirit. 'Independent' was never supposed to mean 'alone.'

While this documentary helps us to understand how culture can be created and modified, I find it particularly illuminating to see how Sweden, its politicians, its leaders and its citizens are openly discussing the problem, rather than sweeping it under the rug. They are not turning a blind eye or kicking the can down the road for future generations. Perhaps their most relevant cultural characteristic is that of facing their problems and finding solutions together. It seems that, for them, there is no other way of doing it, and this may be what I admire most about their culture. Not the perfection that many believe is present in Nordic countries, but rather the ability to reconsider and act accordingly. That is the cultural and personal metaskill that I consider most relevant in order to never to stop progressing.

Instead of clinging to their history, they are applying new ideas. They don't look back in search of scapegoats, nor do they expend time trying to work out where they went wrong. They look to the future and figure out how to do things differently. Will they manage it? I don't know. But if you have the necessary conversations and make plans to try other paths, you are much closer than you were before.

# 9. The cities we live in

I am lucky enough to have lived in four cities that shared some common characteristics while still being very different from each other: Buenos Aires, London, Madrid and Barcelona. I have also spent a lot of time in other cities across four continents, and in each of them, one of the things I have enjoyed most has been experiencing different rituals and ways of celebrating, connecting with people, and exploring the streets and public spaces.

In London, friends play soccer games at the park. To see a professional match, you have to go to a stadium or to the pub for a pint. In Madrid, soccer is played on synthetic grass pitches. Finding a green park is  a rare occurrence, but going to a bar for a drink and to chew the fat with anyone sitting nearby is common. In Buenos Aires, it's rare to spend a weekend without having a barbecue or getting together around the big family table (an Italian throwback, as I understand it) for a plate of pasta and a chat. In Barcelona, they play soccer on synthetic lawns too, and lush parks are few and far between – but the beaches and sea give outdoor life a different vibe. Hordes of tourists flood every street and store, chasing the locals away from certain parts of the city as if it no longer belonged to them, while the mix of languages makes it difficult at times to remember where you actually are.

Cities create contexts, too – they signal to us the things that are valued in each of them, what is possible there, and what is "normal." Essentially, they tell us what is expected of us in order to belong there.

## Legacies

The big western cities we have created and recreated over the last two hundred and fifty years, following the Industrial Revolution, are large-scale examples of a living system undergoing constant transformation. Like countries and societies, cities cannot remain static: if they did, they would stop adapting to the changing needs of their inhabitants and lose their whole reason for existing.

That perpetual flow enables us to reconsider the purpose of cities: what each city invites us to do, what they offer us, and what they ask of us. Each of them has its own systems, symbols and citizen behaviors. The ways people get around, public transport, prices in various zones, businesses, educational areas, parks. All those systems and their physical distribution make our lives easier or harder, and everyone living in any given city is an active part of that dynamic.

The city we live in tells us how the broadest cultural framework operates and offers us the chance to question how this system of belonging influences and impacts us in everything we do. We are its users, workers, shareholders and manufacturers, and we have as much of an influence on the city as it has on us.

One big question I've been asking myself for years is whether modern cities actually help us live the way we want to. In other words, do they help us to flow, to flourish and to develop the best versions of ourselves? It is a question sociologists and town planners ask themselves, too. Do cities, in their current form, make sense? Or does this creation, so necessary for the past few centuries and which has changed to adapt to humanity's changing story, need to be profoundly reconsidered along with our own roles and responsibilities?

We are getting increasingly more tightly packed together, in buildings that occupy every available square foot – and somehow, we are getting used to it. We think it's *normal*. But with the notion of space that we have, with new construction techniques, with increasing connectivity, if we had to go back and create our world again, would we do it the same way? Would we create honeycombs of cubicles measuring three, four, five hundred square feet if we knew that the Covid-19 crisis would not be the last pandemic of even our generation, let alone that of our children?

We have built a world that would probably be quite different if we could go back and remake some of the decisions we have been making for years as a society. I'm convinced that, if we could go back and do it all again with the knowledge we have today, we would do it differently. Of course, we're not going to demolish all those buildings in one fell swoop. That said, in El Poblenou – the area of Barcelona where I live – it seems that that's what they're trying to do! It's what happened twenty years ago, and is still happening today, in Palermo, Buenos Aires, where I grew up and spent much of my life. There, they pull buildings down and build bigger ones, but with smaller apartments. The way I see it, we are exacerbating the problem, rather than trying to come up with alternatives.

In any case, the question is how we modify cities while still living in them. How do we make cities increasingly more satisfactory places to live? Better places in which to lead full lives while undergoing our own processes of transformation (just like what we want to achieve with the organizations to which we belong)?

José Luis de Vicente is a cultural researcher and journalist specializing in innovation, creativity and technology. In a Ted Talk entitled "*La Ciudad Mutante*" (The Mutant City), he explains that the cities we live in are the love children of two technological inventions: cars and elevators. "Before the elevator, the rich lived below, with poor people up in the attic. The elevator flipped that around and added a new dimension to urban spaces, which could now grow up as well as out, exponentially increasing their density. The car renegotiated the distances between home, work and leisure, turning residential suburbs and cities themselves into one space, which was no longer designed for citizens, but rather for millions of rolling exoskeletons made of gas, glass and metal. The cities of the twentieth century grew up and out, like cathedrals. The cities of the twenty-first century are still a mystery."

We tend not to be aware of these factors, because we are born and raised with them. They define our habits and our expectations. To give you a personal example of how this works and how it affects us, I will summarize the sensation of change I felt between the four cities in which I have lived, and how that sensation made me aware of something I had never noticed before.

Having lived in London and spent some time in Berlin, I felt that nature – which I had enjoyed as a child in Buenos Aires – was beneficial to my life. When I moved to Madrid and then Barcelona, I felt something missing: greenery. Big parks, and grass that seems to grow from nowhere. Coming across deer, squirrels and foxes walking around wooded areas of the city and suburbs. I realized that that having a connection with nature affected my ability to connect with the world and with life events.

## Time: the cosmic relationship between nature and Wi-Fi speeds

Living where we live can seem so obvious that we take no notice of its incidence. Take our ability to access nature, given its impact on our ability to connect with the world, evolution, and time. Nature is wise in its rhythms and times, and it teaches us to understand our own processes as human beings. We are part of nature. But that natural wisdom has been relegated in many cities, where bricks and mortar are the central axis, turning their backs on the sea, on rivers, on mountains. We have become disconnected from nature. That has an inevitable effect on the way we are and the things we do.

We live in a world where if something doesn't happen quickly, it's no good. We learn that from the places where we live, too: we have created living spaces and work cultures that deprive us of the wisdom of nature and its processes. Our brains have become accustomed to working that way, too. One of the most common expressions of this – and equally one of the most oppressive – is our relationship with the Internet. A study undertaken by Ericsson labs showed that the (relative) slowness of connection speeds when streaming content elevates users' stress levels and heart rates to similar levels as those of someone watching a horror film or attempting to solve a difficult math problem.

We need everything *now*. But some changes take time, and although we can often speed them up with new technology, practices and innovations, we cannot substantially alter them purely because we want everything *right now*. That belief, characteristic of this time in which everything – results, change, learning – needs to happen immediately, leads us to forget something vital: that when things happen before they are ready to survive on their own, they rarely last. It takes time to strengthen the foundations on which large structures will be built. It happens in construction, it happens with ideas, it happens with the very origin of life.

Allowing mounting anxiety to rush us along is a profound hindrance to the changes we hope to achieve. The sooner we understand this, the sooner we will achieve them. These are paradoxes of life, it's true, but this may be a very important one to resolve.

It happens in modern cities, with complex structures that are not conducive to short-term modification. It happens in Sweden, where social change was more profound and drastic than expected. It happens in large organizations with decades of experience and history. The good news is that there are always counterexamples that show that it is possible, little by little, to initiate deep, lasting change that reconnects us with life on a human level, providing us with some of that natural wisdom.

## An example of change: super-islands

Barcelona's "super islands" (super illas in Catalan) are one such counterexample. Essentially, the idea of the *super illas* was to alter the outline of nine blocks to turn them into one large block around which traffic could circulate under restrictions. If we limit ourselves to looking at the superficial, this seems like a simple modification of street grids in order to create recreation spaces: picnic tables, more trees, and playgrounds where before there were busy traffic intersections. Areas that were previously packed with cars are now full of people chatting, eating together, playing chess and riding bikes with their kids.

How did this process, which fundamentally involved a change in mindset and action, come about? It began with the aim of bringing fresh purpose to life in Barcelona. A new series of intentions. There was a paradigm change in terms of what a city should offer us in order for us to develop there. They went from the old mindset, which said "streets are for cars" to a new model: "streets are for people."

The first thing you have to do is think differently. Then, you have to act differently. This is a great example for understanding how we can bring about change in the system, offering people a new context.

From what I could observe and find out, Barcelona's local government did the following, more or less consistently:

---

**1.** Try, with a reduced group of cases, to gain experience, learn and make the necessary modifications before applying the change on a large scale.

---

**2.** Don't give up at the first hurdle: the initial plan took into account that some new practices wouldn't work, that there would be complaints from other stakeholders (resistance to change is normal), and that they would need to be tolerant in those situations, but without ever doubting in the bones of the plan – no "pilot" is perfect (that's what pilots are for!).

**3.** Draw up a budget in accordance with what's needed for the first test, and then use those results – which underpin the logic, learning and future needs of the process – to secure adequate funding to extend the project's scope.

**4.** Have leaders who are resolute and able to face challenges with both humility and determination.

**5.** Analyze and understand what other parts of the system need to accompany the process of change in order for the whole operation, and the change, to work.

Barcelona is not what it was. It's changing. It lives, grows, adapts. It increases its green spaces and communal areas for its citizens' enjoyment, even in the face of resistance from other stakeholders with different priorities. Anyone who knows about the project knows it has not been perfect and still isn't now. We can even argue over its objective and disagree on many perspectives and viewpoints, but we will certainly agree that it is a good example for discussing and understanding how change can be achieved in line with new intentions.

# 10. The organizations we belong to

In addition to the society we live in and the cities we call home, there is another space of great cultural influence in our ability to develop the best versions of ourselves. As children, school is perhaps the organization with the most influence on us. Our places of work are probably the areas that impact us most as adults: the organizations we belong to and interact with, the place where we spend most of our waking hours, where we invest so much of our time and mental and physical energy. Understanding its dynamics, internal culture, spaces of change and rigidities is key to understanding our own capacity for development.

Like cities, organizations were designed in response to concerns from an era that has now passed. An era when people worked the same job their whole lives and were proud of it. The world has changed, but we have values, practices and levels of awareness that are deep-seated in us but very different from those that newer generations demand. Even companies in Silicon Valley and startups from more than ten years ago may be a few steps behind compared to the speed at which new expectations are generated.

The world is changing in huge strides, and if we believe that we already understand how it works, we will quickly stop understanding it. This will have a direct effect on our abilities and our intentions.

## Organizational culture

First, let's simply define what we mean by *organizational culture*. If we extrapolated everything that defines culture and applied it to a group of people united by a common purpose, organizational culture would refer to those messages that people receive regarding how they should think, feel and act in order to belong to and succeed in that setting.

We create (and modify) organizational culture constantly through the messages we send about what we value. Those messages come in the form of symbols (stories we tell and decisions that serve as examples), systems (from pay to the way we assign budgets), and the behavior of our leaders and mentors.

The problem here is that, when what we say does not correspond with the messages we send out, there is a misalignment of which we can often be unaware but which becomes yet another factor in our immunity to any attempt to change. When we say we value people who try new things and take risks, but we only give opportunities to those who are measured and conservative. When we say there is no room here for people who respond aggressively, but such people occupy positions of power due to their short-term results. When things like this happen, everyone gets the message, loud and clear. It is ultimately more effective to be aggressive or to avoid taking risks in order to get what we want than to try new things or value form above outcome: this is how we create culture with each and every one of our actions.

What you do
speaks so loudly
that I cannot hear
what you say.

Ralph Waldo Emerson

## It's not just about breathing

As individuals, we wonder about the meaning of life and why we do the things we do every day. All organizations were, at some point, conceived in order to solve a problem, respond to a need, or materialize a future aspiration. However, the more they grow, and the more complex and global they become, what those organizations do is no longer necessarily aligned with their initial purpose – sometimes, it is not even aligned with the purpose they say they have now.

A similar thing occurs with companies and teams as with individuals: pressing everyday matters and short-term demands get in the way, we cling to automated practices, and our purpose – the thing that gives us meaning, or at least should! – ends up being more of a wish (or a communication strategy) than anything real.

## From purpose to action

I remember a big transformation project that we undertook for a global insurance company. We worked with over ten thousand leaders scattered around twenty-seven countries, delivering content in fourteen languages. After several months of work, we came to the conclusion that what unified them was too vague. The company had grown through acquisitions, and its image among consumers – just as in virtually all of that industry – was highly negative. They needed meaning to guide them to a new way of doing things. The question we asked them was: How could they have the reputation that they did in a sector aimed theoretically at protecting us when something bad happens, and what would happen if they could change that?

Profit for a company is like oxygen for a person. If you don't have enough of it, you're out of the game. But if you think your life is about breathing, you're really missing something.

PETER DRUCKER

We were not immediately successful, nor was it an easy job, but it opened up deeper conversations which they continued to have for years: the process itself unified them and enabled them to understand that they had to change to redefine industry standards.

And what did they declare as their new purpose? Working towards the progress of people and protecting them when they needed it most. Part of me is proud of having contributed to that, because it is a noble purpose. In addition, it's simple and clear to everyone. It provides direction and expresses the most virtuous part of why, every day, those hundreds of thousands of people get up and go to work together in order to add value to the lives of people they don't know.

The real problem came later, and it evidenced the main reason why many leaders prefer not to enter these processes of change; once they are complete, after months of work realigning what hundreds of people do, the difficult part starts: less talking, and more putting it into action.

That revelation forced them to have intense conversations regarding what they should do in situations considered *gray areas*, where they would previously attempt to justify their decisions with arguable details that favored profits over their reason for existing. This offered a greater sense of security for their customers while still respecting the policies they had signed. This, in turn, generated fresh awareness of what was possible and of what they could produce by integrating the various interest groups. In other words, not just their shareholders (and the executives themselves, with their bonuses) but their clients, too – ultimately, this latter group constitutes the main raison d'être of everything they do. It is only then that it is possible to market companies like this well (and not a moment sooner!), because it means they have placed the consumer at the center of their activity, just as they said they had before.

It's perfectly understandable – recommended, even – to take advantage of our best practices in order to secure new clients. What we must be careful of is that we don't create marketing that exceeds the reality of what we aspire to and are capable of providing. If we are not careful with this, we begin to lose credibility among our customers and interest groups, as well as with our own employees. If you think like a customer, it's suddenly obvious. We don't want anyone to promise us anything they are not capable of delivering. How can we act with increasing awareness of this within our own organizations?

## Creating the culture to shape culture

When you talk about something a lot, but others see no evidence of it happening, a vicious circle often arises: a lot of trendy words, a lot of effort and confusion among teams, and a lot of ways of working that never change. When all those messages and ideas don't materialize, it creates a kind of vaccine that generates antibodies: people have less and less belief in the transformation you are proclaiming will take place, they trust their leaders and corporate messages less, and so they make less effort – albeit subconsciously – toward that change actually happening. This is problematic not just for the change we want to bring about, but for any future changes that may be necessary. That is why, when people don't rally round a suggested change, we look at what has happened in the past that has made them not want (or be able) to trust us too readily, and at how much effort we need to make in order to deactivate those antibodies. If we fail to do this, the desired transformation will not occur at the expected level, and results will continue to be poor. Whatever people have been doing so far will continue to prevail. That's why their practices became habits: they were based on stories that worked and were a sure thing. If we leaders truly want to bring about change, we have to demonstrate again and again that the old ways of doing things will often be counterproductive going forward. The success of any new initiative depends on that. Over the next few pages, we will look at how our ability to reconsider, our commitment to the future (rather than to the past), our willingness to try new things and our inclination to exponentially improve the quality of our conversations are four determining factors in creating a culture increasingly aligned with our objectives, strategy and values.

## Taking a step back to look carefully (at ourselves)

During my college years, I read Gareth Morgan's book *Images of Organization* cover to cover. The author presents eight metaphors: organizations (1) as machines, (2) as brains, (3) as organisms, (4) as culture, (5) as psychic prisons, (6) as flux and transformation, (7) as instruments of domination and (8) as political systems. These *images* helped me to see organizations and systems of belonging from various perspectives and with different logic, and in turn to value the power of metaphors for understanding reality. In this case, it helped me to focus on the great dilemma of change faced by many leaders.

Organizations have an enormous need – and a great opportunity – to reinvent themselves. As we have seen, in order for this to happen, the people working in them must also reinvent themselves. It is a fundamental part of the process. There is no transformation in organizational culture without the transformation of the set of beliefs, values and behaviors of its members, no matter what system we are talking about. The big question is how to change something we are part of – because, without changing the logic we are operating with, it will become an impossible feat.

To this end, it is essential for us to rethink ourselves. One of my aims is to invite you to reflect, before deciding how you can better act and learn from your own experience. The idea is not simply to create a virtuous cycle, but to go a step further: create an upward spiral of continual progress that you cannot leave because it has become a part of you. In short, it can become a better way to live, to create, to connect and to lead.

I fervently believe that leading means transforming. The first step is to look at ourselves from the outside, without judgment, in order to understand what we could be doing better. We need to discover unidentified opportunities to try something different in order to learn and deliver results.

## The dilemma between past success and the desired future

Almost all large organizations hope to be more agile, innovative and flexible. They wonder how they can be more efficient and effective – not just from a technological point of view, but also in terms of how to organize and assemble the people working there and how to help them make better decisions. It's about what machinery to buy, what to do during the pandemic, how to invest, who to hire: decisions that continue to be made by people with their own values, beliefs, concerns and cognitive filters. As a consequence, the ways we all think, relate and make decisions add up to define, to a large extent, the capacity of our organization.

Around fifteen years ago, when talking about culture in organizations, most leaders looked down with a condescending smile before telling us: "Culture? No, that's intangible. It's *soft*. We need to sell more – period," or "all we have to do is implement this new system – we just need someone to come get it up and running." But they would always call us back a few months later, complaining that – for some reason they didn't understand – nobody was doing what the system required. If dozens of safety devices appear overnight in a factory (helmets, floor markings, height safety equipment) with no explanation given for them, how likely is it that people will use them? If a culture considers people who take precautions to be weak, it doesn't matter how many new devices you place at their disposal – no one will use them! A few years ago (and not many), this wasn't called "culture" – it was simply "people don't get it."

It's not hard to guess what happened: culture became the new corporate mantra; all you have to do to get a sense of its influence is look at how the rankings of companies around the world evolved. Some made it because they took this variable seriously; others did so reluctantly (generating a much higher emotional and financial toll); others never even took it into account.

Yes, ideas inspire.
They are fundamental,
and they are also insufficient.
Without action, there can be no
feedback or transformation.

At the moment, there are virtually no leaders who are not wondering how to solve the big problem of individual and collective transformation. When people ask for help with that, I always notice an internal dilemma in them: Why should they take on this challenge when they have been so successful until now? One of the greatest difficulties of our times is actually being able to recognize that the successful habits of the past will not necessarily serve us well in the future. The dilemma is how to acknowledge that, while things we have done so far may have been perfect, they may not be so perfect for the future we desire. And that now, to create a more effective culture for the future, we also need to transform ourselves. All leaders say this, but too many are seduced by *talking* about the concept rather than living it and leading it for real in order to actually make it happen.

If we make announcements regarding the changes to come but then fail to carry them out, we will have the opposite effect to the one we desire. It generates a kind of immunity that will prevent people from believing in our ability to do what we say we will. Maintaining the status quo ends up being the smartest way to prevail.

## Fear of the unknown

On occasions, I have perceived a mix of desires, fears and good intentions, interwoven with the uncertainty of what cultural change is all about but afraid to ask because "everyone's talking about it." We tend to fear the unknown, the new, and the effort involved in traveling an unfamiliar path. That's why extreme behavior sometimes arises: from searching for a magic bullet that accomplishes easy, rapid change, to the sensation that we have all the time in the world and that what we do right now won't make the problem any worse. These extremes have something in common: failed attempts, or results that are both limited and costly. In one way or another, almost without realizing it, leaders end up chasing their tails. As a result, they, their teams and their companies invest more money, time and energy than they need to into generating the transformation they are seeking.

I must admit that this is even more complex for large companies with decades of history, which brings with it deep-rooted processes, leaders with inflated egos, and teams who cruise on autopilot. That said, it happens to newer companies, too – dizzying growth eventually catches up with them, and they find themselves bogged down in the same issues.

In this sense, startups are a threat to older companies: they are starting virtually from scratch, they have no links with the past, they are not clinging to bad habits, and all they have to do is connect with the current problem, their purpose, and their potential future. For this reason, big companies turn increasingly to the strategy of acquiring smaller ones (I could write an entire separate book on how many corporations end up "killing" startups by imposing their own culture on them). Quite simply, these smaller companies are forming their own stories with today's logic and a vision of the future. Some, though not many, still manage to topple giants. Until they begin to run the risk of becoming one themselves. That's why it doesn't matter how big or new a company is. In today's world, the organizations that will prevail are those that are agile when it comes to changing and adapting, and those that make it easy for the people working for them to be a part of the process of change in individual terms and in terms of the teams they make up. In this sense, conversations are key for talking about ourselves and our capacity for change, with no inhibitions or fears and with sincerity and respect.

## The quality of conversations

As leaders of a team, we constantly need to coordinate our actions with others. As such, the objectives we want to achieve are often meaningless if we get stuck in our own heads, with no connection to what's around us or with those who share our microworlds. This interaction is expressed in the form of conversations.

We do it so much that we forget that those conversations are the nets on which we build our fields of action. We are always having a conversation with someone: our friends, relatives, colleagues, bosses, neighbors, or with ourselves, our own minds. We give a voice to the various parts of ourselves so that they can express their perspectives and the different alternatives that cause us to hesitate and analyze things before making decisions.

Within organizations, a great obstacle to change is indeed the difficulty of having those conversations we find awkward. Something as simple as telling the truth with honesty and respect and sharing ideas without fear of reprisals or of being written off as unrealistic, uninnovative, or too "soft." Many organizations dedicate hours, money and effort to resolving this issue. And it makes sense for them to keep on trying, because the quality of conversations changes absolutely everything. So why don't we improve the investments we make in that area at the same time?

How often are our conversations designed to create more trusting relationships and leave every meeting on a better footing than when we went in? How often do we enter conversations in order to convince the other person that our point of view is the right one?

### *Why talk to each other?*

Held back by the culture in which we were raised and to which we belong, we spend every conversation just trying to win. And if we don't win, we want to at least escape the conversation unscathed – as if they were battles to be fought. Sometimes, we enter conversations simply hoping the other person will agree with us (or end up accepting our suggestion), without stopping to understand what they are thinking, what value they might add to what we have said, or even what we can do for them: what they expect from us. We opt for not exposing ourselves or our opinions to scrutiny, let alone changing them, as we believe this to be a sign of weakness.

We want to persuade with our ideas and convince with our plans. It is our way of winning. On top of that, it enables us to dodge the complexity of modifying something and evade the need to understand what other people need or want. Only in exceptional cases do we leaders ask our teams:

What is your objective for this meeting?

For you, what would be a good conversation on this topic?

What do you need to turn these ideas into actions?

Nearly all the customer meetings I attend begin with someone explaining a proposal or laying out a problem (or any other topic that has called us together). Meanwhile, many of those present have checked out. They are all coming from other meetings, where they talked about other topics, or they are simply having a difficult day and are distracted, excited or sad about something totally unrelated to what's going on around the table.

Skipping straight to the content in this way, without exploring the mindset of those listening, produces ineffective conversations: someone is talking and explaining, but few present are really listening.

In order to have productive conversations – where everyone is present in mind, body and spirit – we need to get to grips with a dynamic that changes everything. Before beginning to deliver the content (topic), we must create the context (who, why, where), and – before even that – we must be able to connect with the other people present.

The ability to create cultures where people talk with honesty and respect about what's really going on, what they feel, and what they believe, accelerates the process of improvement and the very process of driving that culture to the next level. The success of these initiatives lies not in our ability to understand them, but in our ability to practice them so much that they become our new way of being and of doing things. They become the new standard of action for everyone involved.

As leaders, colleagues and members of any team, the most relevant question is whether or not we are prepared to have conversations of another nature. If when we say that trust is essential within a team, we are ready to

Connection before context,
context before content.

NITHYA SHANTI

create spaces to build that trust by talking about what is really going on. If not, those conversations will occur behind the backs of those concerned, creating a "water-cooler rumor" culture where there is a lot of talk but very little gets resolved.

My proposal is to change the story we tell for one that enables us to talk about everything. This simply requires the development of some practices we may not use yet – not just because it's most satisfactory for everyone in the long run, but because it is also quicker and more effective when it comes to resolving urgent situations. When connections and trust are established, we can make decisions within minutes and count on everyone's support.

## An example to learn from

How can we align our culture with a new strategy? How can we become more flexible and customer-oriented when we come from completely different worlds? How can we improve the quality and effectiveness of our conversations? What can we do in our next conversation in order to take a step in that direction?

There are always examples we can learn from. Some leaders dive into the murky waters of difficult conversations, letting go of everything that brought them this far but that won't work for the future, and connect with as-yet unexplored methods of work. Some leaders try to understand why the organization they belong to exists today, they think about what different value they can add to the market, they consider that consumers are people living lives full of desire, and that we are all the same in that respect, with our goals, fears and opportunities. Bearing all of that in mind, such leaders do what they can to align their words with their actions. I want to share one such case with you.

People don't care how much you know until they know how much you care.

THEODORE ROOSEVELT

The experience of Joao Adao, current Managing Director of Facebook South America, is an example of this – not just because of his achievements, but because of his journey. I had the pleasure of working shoulder to shoulder with him for many years, and I witnessed his capacity for continuous improvement and the way he led and leads his teams in order to achieve new goals that had seemed impossible. From his years at Yellow Pages to his current position with Facebook, Joao has managed to incorporate practices that enable him to stay one step ahead in any process of transformation. And it's not me saying that – it's his business outcomes and the development of his people throughout all levels, over long periods of time and at more than one company. It's his resilience and capacity for personal transformation, his ability to surround himself with better people without feeling threatened, and his ability to ask for help and to never stop learning.

## Leading stories

*by Joao Adao, Managing Director of Facebook South America*

In 2012, I was invited to lead the digital transformation of the Yellow Pages company in Latin America. Back then, I thought those big books of company details had been consigned to history ever since the Internet became the main way to search for information. But I discovered that the company still had a significant base of two hundred thousand customers who paid to appear in the directories; most were small businesses or microenterprises located outside big city centers.

Hibu, a British company, acquired Yellow Pages due to its great commercial capillarity. Its income was falling rapidly, and the company was short on time to adjust its offering to digital solutions; it was forecast to go bankrupt within a year and a half and would probably have to close down. I accepted the challenge based on this premise: very few companies have the same ability to reach the hyper-fragmented channel of microenterprises, and that provided them with a significant competitive advantage.

During the first few weeks, I quickly realized that the task was going to be much more challenging than I thought; it wasn't just a technical issue, it was a cultural one. It was about the way people had been doing things and thinking for many years. While the company did need to develop digital solutions to help its clients get discovered online where users were increasingly searching for businesses, those products could be obtained without much difficulty through a combination of internal development and strategic alliances with relevant partners such as Google or Facebook.

The problem was the cultural barriers that the company would have to overcome in its process of digital transformation. The first challenge was that the organization had had a monopoly for decades. This had extinguished its cultural ability to learn, innovate, try new things and adjust by experimenting.

Secondly, its processes were not focused on customer satisfaction, even though this was the only possible strategy for us: like any monopoly, the company had previously had the luxury of not placing their customers at the center, because customers simply had no other choice but to use them. Finally, the lack of competition for so long had reduced the company culture's agility and adaptability, two fundamental skills to be able to compete in the new, fast-changing digital market.

We began a process of very profound cultural change, starting at the top, with myself and the leadership team. We worked with the "victim/player"*

* "Victim/player" and "knower/learner" refer to central mindsets in the philosophy and practices of Axialent. They are an invitation to modify the way we explain things going on in the world, and to look at how we interact with those events in order to become more effective. For more information, see: https://www.axialent.com/video/introduction-to-mindsets/

mindset to help us realize that this market change was happening everywhere – it wasn't something that was being done to us, it was simply a natural evolution of consumers' searching habits, and that it was up to us to choose how to respond to that change. We also worked with the "knower/learner" mindset to realize that we were used to believing we had all the answers and would now have to develop much greater humility and open-mindedness to recognize that we did not know this new world, and a new curiosity to learn the new skills necessary for success.

After one of the leadership team's regular meetings in which we spent an entire day analyzing the business and making decisions, I remember that Fran asked me for permission to make a few closing comments before beginning the change process. He expressed his surprise that, throughout eight hours of meetings, we had barely mentioned our customers. He suggested a first activity for helping us understand where we stood: each member of the team would spend a few hours answering customer service calls, so that they could hear first-hand the (many) problems our subscribers were experiencing and develop empathy with their experiences. Not only had they not had this ability to relate to customers before, but the exercise would also help us ascertain whether our teams would be capable of responding to those needs or not.

That experience was a simple, practical way to give us a shot of humility which we always remembered. From that moment on, we began to work with techniques to ensure impeccable commitments, aware that every time someone fails to honor their commitment to another person, it broke the efficiency of the process, generating more work and slowing us down in a market that required high agility. On top of that, it damaged trust between departments, and customers ultimately suffered for all of it.

The hard part of that job lasted around three years. Fran still tells me how fundamental it was that I agreed to go to the call center, that I was an integral part of the process, and – above all – that I wanted to stay one step ahead.

At that point, we had managed to increase the company's profits for the first time after five consecutive years of declines. We reduced the drop in income from the legacy products, accelerated growth in digital products, improved customer satisfaction, and reduced costs by implementing more efficient structures and processes. Today, the company has changed its name in Latin America to "Gurú," and actively supports thousands of small businesses and microenterprises to navigate the new digital world by helping them develop their websites, manage their digital marketing campaigns, and attract new clients to grow their businesses.

I am convinced that none of this would have been possible without the profound work we did on the company's culture more than any other area.

## Starting somewhere

Like the societies and cities we live in, the organizations where we spend a large portion of our lives are a great agent for social transformation, integration and creation of value. Today more than ever, we need that type of company and leader. Similarly, we also need social and political leaders who think and act in this way. The world is undergoing a revolution of collective values – collaboration, ecology, empathy, innovation – that will vanish if we don't practice them. The question, then, is how do we stop dreaming about waking up one day and finding the change has already been made, oven-ready, as if it were something external to us? We have to start somewhere, and that *somewhere* is always easier to find if we try it ourselves.

Paradoxically, the shortest path is to acknowledge that it is a complex and laborious task, and that depending on our own outlook, it may be necessary and gratifying. It's impossible to achieve transformation without being consistent over time and without effort put in by those of us who must lead and implement change in a way that inspires others to be a part of it. In order to achieve systemic change, we must first change ourselves because, when that happens, everything around us is also transformed.

# 11. We make change happen

All human beings have the chance to lead in various places, times and contexts in our lives. Given the culture to which we belong, we often believe and perpetuate the idea that leaders must be perfect. They must know everything and do everything right – almost as if they were superior beings. But even those of us in positions of leadership are still human and therefore imperfect. It's worth remembering this from time to time.

One of the most common beliefs, particularly among those of us responsible for developing and implementing transformation projects, is that it doesn't matter what the change is about or how big it is: we always believe we are facing a type 1 or 2 change, as I described in chapter 6 ("Not all change is equal: the different types of change"). In other words, we believe they are easy or moderate challenges for which all we need to do is listen to a concept or simply decide to do it. This could be a good communication and marketing strategy, but we know that this is not the case when it comes to the actual services and products we offer to the market.

When we look at everything in that way, we run the risk of jumping to the next topic too quickly. We learn to go from subject to subject without necessarily becoming better at the one we are talking about now. And the vast majority of people around us perceive this, too, even if they don't say so.

We become experts in quick but superficial change, without learning any of the topics that require more effort and dedication. What is the impact on the systems we lead? That we will not be able to distinguish between those changes that can be achieved with some training and those that require a longer process.

That's why we encounter so many frustrated leaders and change programs that never achieve their supposed objective: people buy training programs to "be more disruptive," hire a new speaker to "acquire a new mindset," find a new supplier to "learn to have difficult conversations," but without changing the underlying logic or giving time and space to the required practice. They simply hope that this time, doing what has already been done a thousand and one times will produce a different outcome.

This often happens subconsciously, whether because not many people want to enter conflict with the culture in which they are immersed, or because they are afraid that it will involve great personal effort. This leads to the drive for transformation being postponed or boycotted altogether.

As we have seen, talking about things without following through with them leaves a mark. It has an impact. To shout from the rooftops about the changes we need to make is not harmless: it generates effort, financial investment and optimism that deflates over time if we fail to take our commitment to that transformation seriously.

When I talk about transformation, I don't mean type 1 changes (exercising) or type 2 (training), which – to a greater or lesser degree – we can all make happen. I'm talking about profound changes: type 3 (running a marathon) and 4 (playing a new sport), or a combination of both. In other words, a change in mindset, in the way we see and interpret the world, in the tales we tell ourselves to make things make sense, and in the modification of solid habits and behaviors rooted in our personal history or that of our team or organization.

When we talk about cultural transformation, we need to assume the complexity of having to integrate all four types of change into one process, all at the same time.

In every transformation, both organizations and people need to retrain. They must learn to hear and see things that they were previously unable to register, even when they were right in front of them. They have to ingest the necessary information, have an action plan, not give up at the first hurdle, and learn to enjoy the new things, even if they require more effort.

It's important to keep in mind that we will need determination to sustain ourselves, as well as perseverance and a support system that enables us to be consistent. That is the main challenge. And that challenge will determine the difference between achieving it and merely trying to. For this to happen, we need to be convinced and willing to do the work required. I repeat: it is not simple (if it were, we would already be doing it). It is the beginning of a personal process that can lead us to explore uncharted territory. But if we want to take our organization somewhere new, we must first be prepared to visit that place ourselves.

# four

# Be the change

Your kiss became heat, the heat
became movement, the movement
a drop of sweat, the sweat a cloud of
vapor, the vapor wind that nudged
the blades of a windmill in a corner of
La Rioja, where the wine was being
pressed that touched your scarlet lips
[...] Nothing could be simpler, there
is no other way, nothing is ever lost,
everything is transformed.

JORGE DREXLER, "Todo se transforma."

https://spoti.fi/3i0vdCV

# 12. The story of Leda

Leda Wilensky was born March 19th 1925 and died on June 20th 2016, shortly after her 91st birthday. I was in Berlin when Leda died. I had plans to return to Europe and settle down. It would be in Barcelona, although I didn't know that yet.

That morning I was alone, waiting for a meeting of Axialent partners in an apartment a friend had lent me, when the phone rang. I heard the news, and a mixture of relief and sorrow flooded me. Leda Wilensky was my grandmother.

Her family had come to Argentina before World War One, expelled from tsarist Russia. My grandfather had been born at the end of the nineteenth century and emigrated with groups heading for Argentina, thanks to an initiative from Baron Hirsch, a German Jewish financier and philanthropist who led Jewish colonies in America in their escape from the pogroms (attacks against Jews) occurring in Europe. They arrived in the countryside, right in the middle of the prairies of the Pampas, and began working their own land there. They had twenty thousand hectares: an immeasurably huge plot of land, over ninety per cent of which was made up of rocks and infertile earth that made it difficult to take care of cattle. In material terms, nothing was left of all of that. Only their stories, and the stories we create and recreate as their descendants to fill the voids they left behind.

My grandmother Leda had married her uncle, Isaac Cherny. The complexity this created in our family tree (my grandmother is both my grandmother and the niece of my grandfather, which makes her my father's cousin and my second cousin) are barely a stitch in the tapestry of her story. She lived her life in the shadow cast by the harshness and eccentricity of that reborn Russian émigré, who had barely concealed relations with his two nieces, eventually marrying one of them simply because she was the one who fell pregnant.

Over five years, while her uncle-husband lived out a "normalized" family life, Leda gave birth to three sons: my father the youngest of them. Five years after my father was born, Leda was widowed. She was twenty-eight years old, with three children, some land, and a new life ahead of her.

There was a man close to the family. We all knew him as "Chingo." His name was Paulino Barrio and, in theory, he was our grandmother's partner on the land. The official story was that Chingo was my grandfather's accountant and helped him with administrative tasks. Family legend has it that, before he died, my grandfather entrusted him with the care of his wife, children and business. Chingo was one of the most noble, upstanding men I have ever met, and he did so to the letter. For nearly forty years, he was my grandmother's partner, in a hidden, silenced relationship that could not be uttered.

They each lived in their own house but got together every evening to drink tea. Rain or shine, he was always there. Chingo never missed that tea date until the day he died at the age of ninety-eight.

I found out about that intimate life when my sister, eight years younger than me, began to call him "grandpa" one day in all her childlike innocence. That was what she felt he was. And that's when it became blindingly obvious. We all began to wonder and to ask each other, and my parents' only response was to smile. That's when I understood, as if I had been shown the missing piece of the puzzle.

Leda and Chingo made some difficult decisions together, including bailing out during the agricultural crisis of the nineties. They left it all behind, even though the farmland had been their lives. They thought they could use the savings they had to live comfortably for the rest of their lives, but once the sale was finalized, and after a few months of apparent happiness, Leda became sick, and she never got better. Her deterioration was constant for years. My grandmother had bought an apartment in Palermo, opposite my school, where she moved after leaving her historic apartment on Santa Fe Street. Many years later, once she had lost the capacity to decide for herself, my father and his older brother sold that apartment and rented her a smaller one so they could cover her high medical fees: social workers, medication, round-the-clock care. Anything it took to fulfil their promise of never putting her in a home. But things don't always turn out the way we plan.

In the face of her years of intense suffering, the inevitable deterioration that worsened by the day, and her near-vegetative state later on, we almost wished, in a way, that Leda would leave us. It would mean the end of a tragic cycle exacerbated by the deaths of my uncles. At one point, when Leda was in hospital, we were called to see her to say our goodbyes. But Leda returned home. It seemed that death avoided her. I always believed that my grandmother stayed around because she was still mumbling with bitterness, as she had done for all of her adult life: despite her physical frailty, her jaw was set firm, her eyes charged. If we ever made her laugh back when she still recognized us, I have to say that I never saw peace in her eyes – much less any sweetness. There was something she still could not forgive; something that prevented her from looking with gratitude and distance at everything she had been through to create and raise a family all but single-handedly. There was something from her own life that didn't allow her to feel pride or peace about a story that transcended her.

That was until she passed away in June 2016, evoking in all of us that mixture of profound relief and overwhelming sorrow that comes with expected farewells. Leda had finally left this space and time. She was no longer with us, and she had taken with her the stories she had left to tell.

I was hopeful about the possibility that she may have been able to forgive her mother, her father, her husband and her sister, and all those tough years raising three boys who were becoming men somewhere between the fields and the city, marked by a history of which she had been co-creator. Perhaps, at the end, she freed herself of all those burdens. Perhaps, at the end, she was able to look back at her own story with the gratitude and hopefulness of all those grandchildren, with our own stories and with everything that brought us together through being her descendants. Perhaps she managed to make her peace with the love story she *had* been able to choose and which she left to us now that she was gone: the freely given, hidden love of Paulino Barrio.

In that apartment in Berlin, my mind swimming with ideas on how to change several aspects of my life, sorrow was doing battle with relief. It ended in a tie that lasted until I met up with my family some months later and hugged my father, and together, we let her go. It was among those inconsolable, liberating tears that I consciously reassessed the rituals and tales we create in order to say goodbye to the people we love: the same people who allow us to go on living.

## Everything is illuminated

Leda Wilensky left me choked up in Berlin, and hugging my father on our long-awaited reunion. But she also left me endless beautiful, indelible memories that will be a part of the stories of my children, of my siblings' children, my cousins' children, and beyond. They are the stories that shaped us – that made us who we are.

All of us cousins have different memories of our grandmother. She didn't treat us all the same. I think I was one of her golden boys, given the relationship she had with my mother. That was a privilege I enjoyed.

I don't know when it was that Leda had the crazy idea of taking all of us to Disney world, on several separate trips, in the eighties when it was still a novelty and an almost unattainable dream for many children. "When are you going on the trip with *abuela* and which cousins are you going with?"

was the question we all asked each other at every family gathering. It was my turn to go in 1989, for the Fourth of July celebrations. It wasn't until much later that I realized that my grandmother was sixty-four when we went, in 104-degree heat and with leg pain that interrupted our walks, but there she was.

I could see how all of us Chernys rallied around my grandmother and were unified by the trip, during which we discovered a fantastic new world and our first experiences of traveling far away without our parents, getting tucked in by our fathers' mother, who could do anything.

## My grandmother's knishes

A masterpiece. Unbeatable. I'm not exaggerating. To this day, we have not been able to replicate my grandmother's knishes. She had a gift, and many years' practice in the kitchen. Varenyky, knaidlech, borsch and those spectacular handmade potato knishes. She taught us the pleasure of food made with her own hands while talking to us – almost without realizing – about our origins.

Religion never came up in my house, but Leda taught us that we came from Eastern Europe and showed it to us on the map. Years later, I learned that not all Jews ate the things we did, only the Ashkenazi, and that food and traditions have as much (or more) to do with geography as they do with religion.

Above all, Leda taught us to enjoy sitting around the table, celebrating being together. She never shared the secrets to her cooking with us until, by then in a wheelchair, her voice perpetually hoarse, she gave some of us instructions in a masterclass in my father's house. The dough had to be almost transparent so that we could see each other through it, but without breaking, or it would be no good. But we already knew that – it was just difficult to achieve. What we didn't know until that day was her particular attention to one ingredient and how to cook it. That day, we discovered that the key was the exact moment when onion turns golden. That was her secret.

## The chance to be alive

I don't know how well she did it, but I know she did it, and the best she could. With all her imperfections, Abuela Leda gave us life. Not her own, but ours. Here we are, through her strength in bearing Rubén, Mario, and Hugo. For her ability to raise them having been widowed so young and facing so much adversity. For putting a roof over their heads, educating them, teaching them values that made them the best fathers possible – all of that means that today, my cousins and I can keep on telling (and creating) our story.

Even so, these stories are likely to be lost with the passing of the years: to become vague, to take on new hues. Our children's children will be there to keep on rewriting them, and – whether they know it or not – they will be forever connected to the lives of our grandparents. And that is the same for every single one of us.

# 13. The endless challenge

Life is a fascinating journey if we accept that we have everything still to learn. Those of us who learn to run a marathon tend to want to run mountain races after that, and then we go back for more after that. There are always new goals. We are always raising the yardstick we use to measure ourselves and others. Some people train to cut their time down, others to face triathlons or ultramarathons, like the author Haruki Murakami in his essay *What I Talk About When I Talk About Running*. We want to evolve. Outdo ourselves. Find new challenges. Scale new heights.

In this endless process of growth lies our greatest opportunity. The invitation is not merely to learn, but – above all – to enjoy the journey. It is an opportunity to change the story for another: one that says that learning and growing may be the greatest experience life has to offer, and the greatest challenge we can take on each day.

I would bet that most of the ideas I have shared in this book seem reasonable to those of you reading. They are part of what we experience every day, the opportunities and obstacles we all encounter. I didn't invent any of this myself: it is the sum of everything I have learned from working and interacting with a variety of people in different organizations across various countries. They are ideas that almost all of us understand but that we struggle to put into practice. We feel that we could do so much more, but we also feel that we belong to a culture that imposes limits (imaginary, perhaps, but limits all the same) on us as often as it spurs us on. It demands connections from us but creates incentives for us to avoid having difficult conversations. It requires innovation but makes it difficult to do things based on new ideas. It tells us that there is value in vulnerability but makes it easy for those who manipulate others emotionally.

The desire to move forward exists, as does the fear of breaking the mold and feeling exposed. Even with all those limits, the world keeps turning, and if we don't choose to move with it consciously, we will end up being forced to later, when it's unavoidable.

In order for everything we do in life to be more sustainable, enjoyable and effective, the great transformation that we can set in motion is not a specific skill or aptitude. It is the ability to assimilate the notion of change into our daily lives. It is about individuals, teams and organizations becoming more curious, persistent and committed to improvement. And it's about doing that without the need to seem, or be, perfect.

The best way to create the changes we want is to look at each situation and opportunity, each project and each new challenge as an invitation to take the next step. This way, we can enjoy the journey, and our intentions will become reasons to keep going despite the curves, hills and potholes.

We will now delve into a suggestion that can change everything. We are going to connect with a superpower with the capacity to definitively transform absolutely everything we experience: the capacity to transform into our own innovation projects.

To achieve this, the first thing we need to work on is our own axis: we must be able to return to the center at any time.

The key to always finding the next best version of ourselves lies in our ability to learn constantly while we enjoy doing it.

## The wheel metaphor

When I was a kid, I always found it funny when my father would talk about getting "alignment and balancing" for the car every time we were getting ready for a road trip. I didn't know what it meant until I got my own car. Back then, I had no idea that I was learning one of the most important messages of my life: the more requirements placed on us and the more we pick up speed, the more we need to make sure that we are centered – or aligned – around our axis.

Think of life as a big wheel. Like the London Eye, the attraction situated on the South Bank of the Thames, or a Ferris wheel at an amusement park. Imagine that we are at the center of that wheel, and each of the capsules at the ends of its spokes are parts of our lives: friends, family, colleagues, clients, projects, work, and anything that depends on us or on our interaction with them. The spokes connect us to them.

For a while, the wheel turns at a predetermined pace that is more or less constant, but the speed gradually increases and the only way to sustain it is with a central axis. Every new challenge we face makes us feel that the wheel is spinning faster, each rotation more dizzying, and the center that keeps everything moving is having to make an enormous effort to maintain its axis. We are that center. We are the axis that sustains everything that interacts with us and keeps it moving.

Great athletes who achieve their peak performance have the capacity to remain centered and not lose their axis, or to recover it quickly. When I was little, I loved to watch tennis. They were the golden days of Gabriela Sabatini. Her matches against Steffi Graf were spectacular. Gaby's talent always amazed me. But there was something that Steffi Graf had that made her nearly unbeatable: her ability to always be ready for the next shot. She always returned to the center. Today, we see that even more with many of the elite tennis players that dominate the rankings. You don't often see Rafael Nadal, Roger Federer or Novak Djokovic standing still or disorientated after a shot: they quickly get back to where they *should be* to hit the next ball.

You also don't often see the All Blacks, New Zealand's national rugby team–perhaps the best team in the history of all sports in the first twenty years of this century – missing a tackle and looking idly at the ground while the game continues on around them. After five or six attacks by their rivals, in just a few seconds you see there are still fifteen All Blacks standing, defending the whole time. There isn't a moment to lose – even after a slip, the key is to get center-stage again immediately, ready for the next play. This is what the teams who manage to beat them mostly did, and they had to be able to do it while playing against them, to near-perfection for the whole game.

In squash, the symbolic potential of this is crystal clear: the player in the center is the one who dominates the game, as well as being the one who runs the least and doesn't get exhausted. I know, because I find it hard to be in that place, and that's how my friends – who are less fit than me and don't handle a racket so well – manage to destroy me game after game.

Our ability to get back to the center is a fundamental part of bringing out the best version of ourselves – it's about not overthinking things when something doesn't go the way we expected, and being able to immediately connect with the best place to be for our next step. Getting back in the game and focusing on what the "next play" requires of us to give it our all at the next available opportunity.

The moment of action is not the ideal time to think about what went wrong. There will be time for that later, when we will have to ask ourselves the right questions and draw up a strategy for improvement. While the game is still in play, the focus needs to be on the next move, never on what just happened.

## Stop resisting

Being connected and centered means accepting that what is happening is happening, and that resisting it won't make it disappear but merely strengthen it. Being present means interpreting what is going on as information and flowing with it without judging it. When we judge and categorize it, we allow our brain to invest time in resisting it, rather than getting back up, centering ourselves and getting ready for the next tackle.

We resist things that happen as if by simply doing so they would go away. The moment we accept what's happening, we are able to focus our energies on actively deciding what to do in a way that is aligned with our values and intentions. Otherwise, we are simply reacting, not responding. In general, reacting doesn't bring out the best version of ourselves but rather the most rushed version.

Stress is the expectation that what is happening right here and now, shouldn't be happening.

The ability to be present in every sense in what is happening, in what we are doing, and in what we decide, is the experience of being 100% connected to the present moment. That connection with life events, whatever they are, turns each moment into an opportunity to get back to our center. This way, we will always have the chance to do things a little better than last time.

Understanding, embracing and appreciating this possibility can inspire us to make every situation into an opportunity to be grateful for what has happened. When the unexpected happens or things don't turn out the way we planned, our hearts beat faster, which tells our brain that something is "wrong." Something we thought we could control has become uncontrollable. So, our minds bring our fears to the forefront, our hands begin to sweat, and the person who is there – giving a presentation, taking an exam, or whatever – is no longer us, but an accelerated, unfocused version of us.

Bringing the best versions of ourselves into the world is not a definitive state – it is a constant practice that accompanies us our entire lives.

The best way to escape this and get back to the center is to help calm our minds and bodies. To do that, we need to breathe normally. Sometimes, it's as simple as taking a minute to stop and breathe. That act alone changes everything. It's like hitting the reset button on our system. That is what our brains do when we take a moment: it connects us, helps us look at the situation objectively, and offers perspective. It can even help us find the good in the most adverse of circumstances.

When we breathe, our minds are stilled, our blood circulates more calmly, and we gain perspective. When we look at ourselves from afar, we gain awareness of what we are doing and we can recover from the inner storm we were in the middle of for a moment. In the process, we gain nothing from trying to appear perfect and hide the fact we have tripped – we will always trip, and most of the time it's obvious! We can always improve our ability to recover faster, until, one day, we barely realize we are doing it.

> After watching the sensei Morihei Ueshiba, founder of aikido, practicing with an experienced fighter, a novice student said to him: "Master, you never lose your balance. What is your secret?" The sensei replied: "I am constantly losing my balance. My skill lies in my ability to regain it."

# **14.** Learning to change

We live in a world that increasingly requires agility, innovation, flexibility, and the ability to learn new logic and techniques, regardless of our age. In addition, we are living longer and longer, and the consequence of this is quite obvious: much of what we know today will be insufficient in the near future.

There is an essential skill that helps make all change a little easier, more enjoyable and more effective: learning to change. We need to develop a more "natural" way of evolving so that it becomes a way of life rather than an effort. Like breathing. We need the ability to change and learn to become a part of who we are and what we do.

That's when everything changes – for us and for the way we are and the way we do things. Because we will be the same and yet not the same. Because we will have acquired a *superpower*. A power that helps us develop skills we do not have today, and to rescue those intentions we talked about at the beginning of this book: the values and actions that make us feel proud of ourselves and that lend meaning to our journey.

This superpower is made up of some essential ingredients which we have to find and develop:

Being present.

Nourishing ourselves.

Showing appreciation and gratitude.

Doing *the right thing*.

Connecting with other alternative perspectives.

Believing that we can always, always improve.

## From anticipation to the present moment

The eagerness to get what we want right now is almost pathological in today's world. We see it in the younger generations and their relationship with technology, but also in ourselves, the adults who have spent much of our lives moving at a different pace and now become irritable if we ever have to wait more than five minutes for service in a store or restaurant.

Life always surprises us with the unexpected, and even knowing this we still find it hard to live with that constant uncertainty. Our minds won't let it go and they interrupt us constantly, as if agitation were the solution. But as soon as we resolve something, we are already looking to the next thing, and we get frustrated if we don't achieve it right away. It's a vicious circle that often becomes routine and subconscious.

I may talk about connection and about being present in the moment as intentions for expressing the best version of myself, but I can't tell you how often I pull out my cellphone during dinner with other people, whether to check my messages or because someone asked a question and my automatic response is to google it. That's my ego, relegating my virtuous self to the screen, because when I look up, the conversation has moved on. When

Anxiety is our mind going faster than the speed of life.

Anonymous

that happens, I realize that I missed something much more important than the perfect answer I was trying to provide. I missed part of the conversation. People's expressions. The precious chance to be with other people and share with them. It's a moment: the blink of an eye. But it all counts, and it's all practice.

## Everything can be nourishing

Our whole lives, we learn to escape the present moment in order to avoid difficult feelings. We turn to autopilot when asked how we are, and answer with "fine, thanks." We even answer ourselves in that way. Why? Because it is hard for us to look at what's going on here and now, and whatever brought us to where we are. If we think about all the things we consider "bad" in life (losses, failures, unexpected changes in course, disappointments), we see that they are a part of our stories and part of what made us who we are today. Everything that happens in our life is the fruit of those turning points that we call "difficult situations." But we are only able to see them for what they are after some time has passed and we have gained perspective.

Developing the ability to recognize how beneficial this is at the point in which something is happening is a real challenge. It is the way we begin to connect with the lessons that a normally negative feeling or emotion can teach us – like sadness or pain – and it is an opportunity to enjoy momentary achievements for what they are: momentary. That connection is critical to becoming better prepared for the future.

The episodes in my life I most remember today, the sharpest, most vivid ones, are those where I was 100% connected to what I was feeling. Many such moments were not what I would call "happy." Of course, some feelings are more pleasant than others. For example, anger makes me uncomfortable, but I have learned that it is a good source of information for knowing when something bothers me. That simple act of getting some distance from my own story and looking at it objectively rids me of my anger: I start thinking about why I am angry and what I want to do about it. That subtle difference in awareness changes everything, for me and for those around me.

## Appreciation and gratitude: two essential ingredients

Overwhelmed by routine, by our modern lives, we lose perspective. We don't always remember that we likely form part of the tiny percentage of the world's population that is highly privileged: if we have a roof over our heads, food on the table every day, access to education and the ability to buy a book, we are among the five to ten per cent of people with the most resources out of the more than seven billion people living on Earth.

We subconsciously take it for granted and assume our lives are the norm. Our problems are reduced to whether we can get another point of market share, win an argument, or get online fast. We forget how we got to where we are, and we forget everything we have. That's why the ability to look at ourselves objectively and gain perspective helps us in our evolution process: it gets us out of the confinement that is our own story, enabling us to transform the way we see ourselves and everything we have, everything we have achieved, and everything that has been given to us. It also gives us perspective on what we want to do faced with this information, and the knowledge that we have opportunities that many do not.

Gaining perspective reconnects us with what's important to us because it reduces our adrenaline and gives us the space to look at ourselves from the outside, thus enabling us to *act* differently. And there is a clear difference between doing things from a place of gratitude and appreciation and doing them with the sense that we are lacking something, that something was not "given" to us. Knowing this drives us to behave more like protagonists. Essentially, it gives us the capacity to connect with the world with appreciation and gratitude. Saying thank you, acknowledging others, valuing the challenges that appear while knowing that they are often "first world problems," as I was once told by Raj Sisodia, founder of the Conscious Capitalism movement.

To help people to connect with this practice, there is a video I often use when working with teams. It demonstrates all the good things that are happening around us and that our minds have stopped noticing. If you search "365 grateful" in any Internet search engine, you will find the experiment performed by the photographer Hailey Bartholomew, inspired by practices we can all do in order to connect with a part of ourselves that we often disregard but which, in fact, changes everything.

It is incredible how simply being aware of this can change our whole day. It is worth trying, even just once, in order to see how it changes the way we treat others and the weight we give to certain situations. We can experience how, if we change our outlook, the world changes too. Often, it takes a weight off our shoulders and the weight we place on the shoulders of others.

This is a constant exercise. From going to a meeting and thanking someone for having made a contribution that otherwise went unnoticed, listening without interrupting or offering unsolicited advice, or simply keeping our promises: all these gestures connect us to another kind of energy. Once we can do that, it becomes an everyday practice until our brains retrain themselves to work in this way. This keeps working until there is no turning back, because a better version of ourselves has emerged.

## The power of the mind: what you practice grows stronger

Shauna Shapiro has been a professor in the graduate department of Counseling Psychology at the University of Santa Clara, California, for more than fifteen years. She has worked extensively on training the mind and body. Her studies show that changing our "internal landscape" – the way we see and feel what is going on by training our minds, hearts and bodies – can alter our levels of happiness, gratitude and connection with ourselves and others.

Shapiro's research helped to spread the notion of *neuroplasticity*: our brains can be trained and modified like any other muscle. The only difference is that this muscle drives and influences everything else. It is the big computer of the system that we are.

When I worked with her, one of the greatest discoveries I made was realizing the belief that we are only training and practicing what is good, what is virtuous, what makes us better people. We believe that, by practicing a new exercise for an hour and doing the opposite for the rest of the day, that hour we consciously invest will generate a greater effect than everything else. In reality, we are always practicing. We are constantly exercising our minds and reinforcing something: an idea, a behavior, a reaction. Everything we do is practice that reinforces the way we do things and the way we are – and that happens when we are not doing that which we consider virtuous, too. In one of her most popular Ted Talks, Shapiro explains how she had this revelation during a meditative experience in a monastery:

"I was unable to talk to the monks about my struggles. [...] I started judging everyone around me, even the monks: Why are they just sitting here? Shouldn't they be doing something? Fortunately, an English-speaking monk arrived from London the next day and I was able to speak with him. [...] he responded with a heartfelt chuckle: "Oh dear, you're not practicing mindfulness. You're practicing judgment, impatience, and frustration."

If we are constantly training our brains, then we need to keep helping it to practice the things we want: the things that are good for us and make us more virtuous. And if we look at it that way, everything is an opportunity to learn, because that's what our brains are doing right now. The sooner we see that, the sooner we can bring our best intentions to life along with the best of us and what we want to be in every space in which we interact, whatever the role is that we are being asked to play.

## Connecting with other perspectives

Alvin Toffler said that the illiterate of the twenty-first century would not be those who could not read and write, but those who could not learn, unlearn, and relearn. In that same vein, Fred Kofman explained that we have different ways of looking at the world, and that one of the most virtuous and effective ways was that of the "player" (as Joao Adao explained so well when sharing his case) and the "learner." Let's look in depth at what Fred said about this: "Knowers claim to know how things are, how they ought to be, and what needs to be done. They give a lot of orders and ask very few questions. On the other hand, learners are curious and humble, less certain about how to interpret what is going on and what to do about it. They are more inquisitive than directive. They tend to consider others' perspectives instead of imposing their own." It's as simple as making the most of the knowledge of different people and systems in order to make better decisions, rather than wanting to show who knows more and making decisions guided by our egos. Our egos always believe they are right, even when evidence indicates otherwise.

There is a phrase from American writer and philosopher Eric Hoffer that connects with these mindsets:

In a time of drastic change, it is the learners who inherit the future. The learned usually find themselves equipped to live in a world that no longer exists.

We all know people who found it difficult to achieve something yet managed to make progress and changes simply because they connected with the idea of evolution through the humility of acknowledging their own limitations and seeing them for what they were. They managed to defy their own view of themselves and change their mind about their own skills. All of this begins with our capacity to perceive the world, with what we choose to think when challenges arise, and who we want to be in our interactions with others.

I invite you to consider that perhaps we have a little of everything, and if we do not recognize the knowers within ourselves – those egos that feel good about knowing things, defending their ideas to death and winning arguments – we will find it hard to effect real change. So how do we make ourselves better learners and teach our brains to smile more and enjoy learning more than winning debates?

## There is always, always room for improvement

Carol Dweck, a professor of Social Psychology at Stanford University, coined a concept to refer to this mentality: *growth mindset*. This explains the impact of believing in the idea that all human beings can always get better. Dweck tells us: "I heard about a high school in Chicago where students had to pass a certain number of courses to graduate, and if they didn't pass a course, they got the grade "Not Yet." And I thought that was fantastic, because if you get a failing grade, you think, I'm nothing, I'm nowhere.

But if you get the grade "Not Yet" you understand that you're on a learning curve. It gives you a path into the future."

Our brains, our histories of socialization, and our systems of values, beliefs, education and everything surrounding the ecosystems to which we belong, have reinforced the belief that our skills are set in stone and that our intelligence is set and difficult to change beyond a certain age. We tend to define people by attributing qualities to them, as if these were fixed. We stereotype each other. This means that we stop studying and practicing new things that could not only make us better at them, but that we could also simply enjoy. This is the difference between seeing ourselves as a static image on a loop, always showing the same picture, and seeing ourselves as constant works in progress with pictures that change all the time.

Dweck says that language contains a key piece to helping us modify the stories we tell ourselves: the word *yet* is essential, and the more we use it with ourselves and others, the more spaces and contexts we create to let everyone know that we can always get better. That nothing is fixed. That we are constantly changing, and that we have the capacity to keep learning and improving forever.

I am well aware that I will never play tennis like Federer or soccer like Messi. I will never play the guitar like Paco de Lucía or paint like Dalí. However, I have no doubt that if I practice what I want and what matters to me – what brings me satisfaction or pleasure – my skill will improve and tomorrow I will be able to do better than I can today. The mere act of taking tennis lessons once a week and playing with a friend on one other day for just three months brought me to a level I had not achieved in ten years. I would find it pretty hard to win a point against Federer, but I understand that it is not my game, nor my league. In the same way, Federer – or any of our idols in sports or the arts – would not be able to do well at some of the things at which we are highly trained. We can all do something better than the rest, and we owe much of that success to our hours and hours of practice.

## Tibetan singing bowls

A few years ago, Nithya Shanti gifted me two Tibetan singing bowls. I always enjoyed their sound and their ability to achieve harmony with their surroundings, and even to create silence with their sound. For me, they were untouchable, faraway artefacts, that I planned to use only when Nithya visited me. One day, I began to imitate what I had seen him doing with them. I chose the smallest one, placed it in the palm of my hand, took the mallet with the other, and stroked it in circles at varying intensity to see if the bowl let out any sound. Nothing. Nothing at all. I left it there.

A week passed. Then another. Then another. I felt challenged and somewhat embarrassed to own such a priceless instrument and use it only as an ornament. Every time someone visited my house, they would admire the bowls and ask me if I knew how to play them. I never wanted to admit that I didn't know how to make the beautiful bowls sing. One day, having taken one in the palm of my left hand and rotated the wand around it, it finally made a noise! I was filled with joy and inspiration, and it galvanized me to keep trying. Today, although I do it absolutely imperfectly, I can caress the bowl with balance and make it sing, at least for a few fleeting minutes. I am sure that it sounds a little better each time.

We can use every situation to demonstrate what we know, or we can use it to learn everything that we don't know yet. We always have the option to experience any situation, challenge or experience as a space for exploration and progress. It's up to us.

## The (difficult) first step

There is a situation common to many people I work with during these processes. We want to make a change: to improve and evolve. We understand that we need to. After some reflection and analysis, we are ready to do it. We have decided, and we have that initial enthusiasm. But we often do not know how to take the first step, and we get stuck. That conundrum can be a barrier to initiating the process of change. That's why it is often so important to be able just to take the first step. I remember a study that explained that if you want to go to the gym in the morning, work out and get in shape, but you find it difficult to get out of bed, you should not focus on the long-term vision but rather on the next step: getting out of bed and putting your feet on the floor, then putting on your workout clothes, then going out into the street. Every step gets you closer to the next, and the whole thing becomes much more effective. Being able to take that first step is fundamental.

Of course, as I have mentioned at various points in this book, I don't believe in universal methods. Every one of us is a different person, going through a particular life situation and needing different things. For each specific need, there are several options to explore, to do, to try. What *is* universal is that if we dare to try something, we will be that much closer to discovering what works for us and how to make it happen.

These last few years, I have helped many people begin that process and overcome that first hurdle, and none of them have ever regretted the experience. This in mind, I want to share two examples of processes I have tried with different clients, and which have always been positive in helping them to turn into people who dare to innovate within themselves.

A focus on the Immunity to Change, as taught at Harvard, is based on a constructivist theory on development and is the result of years of research in areas of work related to business, the government and education. Its purpose is to help people effect personal or professional changes that they have unsuccessfully tried to make before. Lisa Lahey and Robert Keagan developed this methodology, combining our capacity for thought, understanding, action and learning. I have tried it on myself and on hundreds of leaders, and it always has a positive, transformative effect. This focus provides a mirror in which people can see how they are subconsciously sabotaging their own quest for change in pursuit of feeling secure and safeguarding something they consider valuable.

These hidden compromises are nothing to be ashamed of – they are a part of us that is on the alert and seeks to protect us. The focus enables us to use a new perspective of ourselves and our basic assumptions in order to create new paths to lasting change.

Oseas Ramírez Assad, former Cisco Systems executive and current partner at Axialent, is an expert in the innovation and development of ecosystems that allow people to innovate in products and services. He has been working with many of us for several years, trying and improving on the Optimal Me method in real-life situations based on the following conundrum: instead of procrastinating and talking about something, how can we simply try it out and see what we learn from the experience, becoming more and more innovative within ourselves?

Exploring that question led him to reconnect with his years of psychological training and analyze some aspects of the science of behavior. At the intersection of these sciences with innovation, he discovered an opportunity to experiment with many areas that have a tremendous impact on people's quality of life: How can we improve our physical, mental and emotional health? How can we increase our effectiveness by aligning our values and desires?

At first, he thought those areas had already been explored to death. A simple Internet search throws up examples of tips, hacks, guides, tools and gurus who promise the mechanism or system for achieving that sought-after well-being, superior performance, or any other thing we may want. There is a long list of people who have put this enormous pledge to the test and failed to effect lasting change. Ramirez Assad was one of those people. He asked himself similar questions to those posed by Lisa Lahey when she developed her Immunity to Change method: Why, knowing that things are good for us, do we still not do them? Why do we find it so hard to implement successful changes when we know they will have a positive impact on us?

The search for the answer to this led him to create the process Optimal Me, as a program in which people design personal experiments and learn to carry them out methodically. He has run this program in over ten countries, and we continue to learn from it with every new group or client. Some executives have improved their cognitive capacity and concentration by trying out intermittent fasting. Others have explored the possibility of saving time with their teams by eliminating the need to deliver reports, by designating weekly no-meeting days, and promoting meditation as a pillar of well-being.

These are but two examples I have found effective for getting ever closer to transformation in innovative projects. You can find out more about these and other methods, with testimonies and reflections from their creators, on my website (www.francherny.com). There are probably many other processes that they have experienced that have helped them and that many others can try. Always remember that the most important thing is taking the next step: "getting out of bed and putting on your workout clothes."

# 15. Let's play Tetris

As a child, I used to play a game that I found impossibly challenging: Has anyone ever actually won at Tetris? The answer is no, simply because it is a never-ending game. As we get better, we move up to the next level, and then the next. All we are doing is acquiring the skills needed to pass each level and take on a new challenge. It wasn't until I was an adult that I discovered that the game's message serves as the perfect example for transformation in innovative projects.

Living life, exercising some form of leadership, forming an active part of an organization or ecosystem: all of this creates new levels of challenges. Although it can be difficult to see it, they are nothing more than invitations to grow, change, learn, evolve and develop. To transform, when what we know, are and do is no longer enough for us. To challenge our own stories and beliefs and find the person we want to be. To bring to life the best version possible of ourselves on the next level of the game we are playing, and get ready to play the next one up, which is right around the corner. And the best thing we can do is learn to play better each time, with the awareness and conviction that real challenge is to play the game, never to win it.

We already know we will lose life's final battle. But with this knowledge, that finiteness can be our greatest advisor: it reminds us that, since the end is inevitable, the best thing we can do is enjoy the journey, so that when we reach the end of it, we will be able to take a deep breath and smile knowing that we gave it our best and that we helped those around us to do the same.

This is my great invitation: to live life focused on making this journey an unforgettable experience. It is a lesson we can spend our entire lives learning.

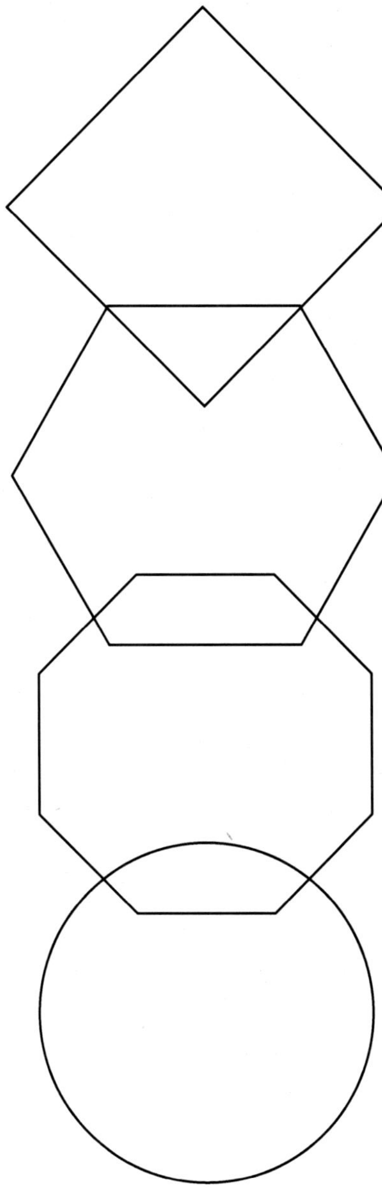

# epilogue

On this journey of experimentation and constant challenges that we call life, as we grow and get older, we are more and more interested in the idea of leaving behind something that transcends us. A legacy. For some people, that could be their children and family; for others, it may be about leaving behind an extraordinary idea, lasting inventions or indelible memories through expressions of their art.

This idea of transcendence as a form of realization spurs us into action. We spend our lives worrying about achieving all kinds of different things, but in our hearts, what we want is to leave something we consider relevant and valuable, and for it to outlive us.

We never know when the end will come, but we do know that when it happens, we are unlikely to be thinking about profitability in this year or that year, or how we did in the last sports tournament, or how many new clients we acquired in our best year. All of that is part of the here and now, but it will be dust in the wind one day. That is not our greatest legacy.

## Lead to transform

In his book *Legacy: 15 Lessons in Leadership*, James Kerr analyzes how a group of sportspeople, against all the odds, ultimately laid the foundations for what is now the most successful sports team in the world: the All Blacks, New Zealand's rugby team. The book's title refers to a tradition that they began and which was part of their significant cultural change in terms of the values, ideas and behaviors they needed: the team jerseys are passed from player to player. This ritual, symbol and story involves players who retire handing their jersey to a new player. But it's not just a generational handing down – when they then pass that jersey on to the next player, it must have more value than when they inherited it. That is a commitment they make when they receive it. That is what they consider to be success. The pride of knowing that each generation fights to add value to something others have already added to. It integrates the past. It gives meaning to the present. It builds a future.

As I mentioned before, I strongly believe that to lead is to transform the ecosystems to which we belong – our friendship groups, families, companies, and work or sports teams – so that the people around us can find the best versions of themselves, too.

We all play a leadership role in one or more of those ecosystems. We can all have an influence, model behavior and make decisions that impact others. And we can all do it with humility and with the knowledge that we, too, are experimenting and evolving. Recognizing this is a turning point for transforming into adaptable people, more human and more committed to our dreams and intentions.

To lead is to connect with what we are passionate about, and to invite others to believe. It is to inspire. It is to find a way to make everything more than the sum of its parts. It is to create spaces where everyone, including ourselves, can live out each situation in line with our own values in order to express the best versions of ourselves.

If we want to "stay alive," perhaps the most effective route is to work on ridding ourselves of the armor that is our ego. Making ourselves dispensable and creating the right conditions for things to work when we are not there. Being able to construct cultures and lead by example so that others can do things for themselves. So that, in the face of each new challenge, everyone can find a new way to develop their capability.

It's what we all say we want for our children, our friends, our loved ones, the colleagues we value, the next generation: the idea that when we are gone, they will be ready for the challenges still to come.

When everything (and everyone) can work well without us, that may be the closest we can get to success.

## The next opportunity

This book is, in essence, an invitation to live mindfully. To accept life's uncertainties. To go from adaptation and change forced by circumstances to progress and transformation with meaning. To view each situation as a preparation for the next level, aligning everything we do with our best intentions. To use all the resources at our disposal to be a better version of ourselves every day. In every conversation, every project, and every fresh challenge.

It is in this space and time where our deepest uncertainties are born, and so too are our greatest opportunities.

Who do I want to be when life presents me with the next challenge?

# Acknowledgements

The journey of writing this book has gone far beyond the moment I made the decision to put my thoughts and experiences down on paper. It was a turning point that involved experiences from my childhood, through my adolescence, and every experience connects with so many people from all walks of life. That is why I would firstly like to thank my parents, who always instilled in me that appreciation for diversity and the enjoyment of connecting with other people. Thanks also to my siblings and my lifelong friends, who have been witnesses to and part of my own process: my changes, my doubts, my progress and the circumstances that, one way or another, changed my course.

I also want to thank all the leaders of the teams and organizations whose confidence, words and experiences have inspired and driven me, in the best sense, to want and need to keep learning every day, as well as to lead my own organization and the teams to which I belong. To all of you who see themselves reflected in the pages of this book, I say a resounding "thank you" that is full of fondness and gratitude.

Over the next few paragraphs, I would like to name more specifically some of the people who have played an active part in the construction of these pages, dedicating their time and energy to it.

Joao Adao, Lisa Lahey, Paulo Pisano, Oseas Ramírez and Agostina D'Alessandro – thank you for contributing your experiences, texts and ideas to enrich the first edition of this book. Thank you to Raff Viton for generously inspiring the title of this book with his ideas and our work together. To Cony Flores, Guillermina Maier, Juan Fernando Posada, Alejandro Lorusso, Agustín Beccar Varela, Lucía Suárez, Caro Cherny, Javier Argüello, Richi Gil and José Suárez, for playing an active role in how these pages are written. Some through having been part of the inception of this process by sending me their personal reflections on their experiences of working together, and others for the enormous task of reading manuscripts that were nowhere near this final edition. This book was made possible through your honest, tactful critiques and the best intentions to help me express the best version of myself.

A huge thank you to Nithya Shanti for all his teachings, for his friendship, his humility and his gratitude. So many years of doing things together have undoubtedly made me a better person by showing me practices that help me to find the best version of myself from a place of appreciation and gratitude. And to the other members of Axialent's Academic Committee, Shauna Shapiro, Raj Sisodia, Jorge Valdano and Bill Withers, who – along with Lisa Lahey and Nithya Shanti – not only trusted in my leadership and vision but also brought me unique experiences in every area of their expertise that have helped me to grow and expand my ability to help our clients.

Here, I would like to highlight the work of all my colleagues at Axialent, who have also been part of this journey in various ways, presenting me with challenges that have helped me to grow and learn each day. Many thanks to all those who were and have been part of this community of people so committed to their work and to our common purpose, who have kept us united even in times of crisis and through a pandemic, making an effort which called for solidarity and commitment to add value to our clients, showing that this is much more than just our job. It is a commitment to an idea, to common values and to a way of life.

A huge thank you to Flor Grieco for all her work with me on this process, to Joaquin Mirkin and Dario Helman for having contributed to pushing me into action. To the PAM! team for having accepted the challenge and found creative ways to help me finish these pages when Ona and Valentín decided it would be better to come into the world a few weeks earlier than expected.

Finally, I want to thank my dear Gemma, who – even without knowing what would become of all this when it all began some eighteen months ago – never doubted for a moment in supporting me along every step of the process. A process which has been both creative and full of reflection, questions and change: an introspective process that has led us to change a few things in our own lives, and which has only been possible due to her unending openness and solidarity.

Thank you. Thank you. **Thank you.**

In maps of the sky the sun
always shines / and the rain and
the clouds have to cover their eyes.
The green grass is a faraway
blanket / you can't escape it,
just fly and you'll get there.

TOQUINHO, "Acuarela."

https://spoti.fi/30JQA59

*Be the change* was printed in February 2022
at Imprenta Dorrego (Av. Dorrego 1102),
Ciudad Autónoma de Buenos Aires, Argentina.